AF413144

KERRY SUTHERLAND

An Eye for Genius

James Brand Pinker and Henry James

Portions of this material have been previously published in The Henry James Review and The Henry James E-Journal.

First edition

ISBN: 9798218173548

Cover art by Diren Yardimli

This book was professionally typeset on Reedsy.
Find out more at reedsy.com

Contents

An Unlikely Partnership

When literary agent James Brand Pinker died of influenza in February 1922, the *New York Times* reported that "among the authors whom he represented in this country were Henry James, Joseph Conrad, John Galsworthy, Frank Swinnerton and Compton Mackenzie"[1] and the London *Daily Mail* noted "he was a close friend of Mr. Henry James."[2] James died six years before Pinker and the other authors listed in the *Times* were very much alive, so the decision to place James's name first, along with the *Mail* claim that James was a friend rather than a client, speaks to Pinker's importance in James's life and the awareness of that relationship in the publishing world.

Henry James and James Brand Pinker seem an unlikely pair. The established middle-aged American author, long an expatriate living in England, France, and Italy, and the tough-minded Scottish literary agent appear to have little in common. Pinker's policy as outlined in the 1901 *Literary Year-Book and Bookman's Directory* was "of helping young authors in the early stages of their career, when they need most the aid of an advisor with a thorough knowledge of the literary world and the publishing trade."[3] The directory entry fails to mention the

---

[1] "James B. Pinker Dies Here." *New York Times* (10 Feb. 1922): 13.

[2] "Literary Agent's Death." *Daily Mail* (10 Feb. 1922): 5.

[3] "Agents - James B. Pinker." *Literary Year-Book and Bookman's Directory* (1901) 118.

agent's pursuit of authors with symbolic or cultural capital; James, of course, would fall into that category, and while he had managed his own business affairs for decades with occasional assistance from family and friends, the complications of the turn of the century literary marketplace along with a variety of personal factors created the need for a permanent and proficient advisor such as Pinker advertised.

The magazine market grew exponentially as the year 1900 approached; the abolishment of paper taxes earlier in the century lowered prices, and the demand for cheaper reading material rose alongside this development as the Education Act of 1870 in England and continued efforts towards compulsory education in the United States (a longstanding affair from 1645-1918) created an increasingly literate public. The advent of the transcontinental railroad in the United States in the 1860s widened the distribution area as it increased the speed at which material was delivered. The invention and use of linotype beginning in 1884 allowed for faster typesetting of these materials.

By 1894, inexpensive single volume prints and reprints had replaced the triple decker novels that filled the shelves of circulating libraries, offering access to readers who could not afford the larger versions. Publishers promoted their authors and titles by advertising them in trade journals, newspapers, and magazines, and aimed to keep as much profit from the authors' work as possible to cover this investment. They also had in-house serial outlets with which to test the market before printing an author's work in book format, such as *Harper's Bazar* and *Scribner's Magazine*.

Authors were used to a half profits system in which they shared earnings equally with publishers, which kept them waiting for money until after the publisher took his share to cover expenses and created complications if they expected a greater and more timely reward for their work. The literary agent, as James Hepburn notes, was an "inevitable phenomenon,"[4] appearing on the literary scene informally around 1875 to represent the authors' interest when dealing with publishers. Authors were often at a disadvantage by their lack of knowledge about the market and the potential profit inherent in their work, and needed the business savvy of an agent who would bargain on their behalf. As Mary Ann Gillies notes, "agents undermined publishers' traditionally dominant position by forcing them to expose their activities to public scrutiny - public in the sense of authors and agents. They helped authors empower themselves - by assisting them in their fights for better financial terms and more control over their literary property."[5]

The half profits system, in which authors shared the financial risk with publishers, gave way to the leasing rather than outright sale of copyrights on the basis of a percentage of royalties and an advance on those royalties. A shift in power from publisher to author was possible through the mediation of the literary agent, and while James had successfully negotiated his way through a variety of publishers, the expansion of the market along with his failure to adhere to a trade courtesy that required faithful relationships with the same publishers created business problems he was unable to manage on his own.

His refusal (inability) to write on demand, meet deadlines, and cater to the changing preferences of a growing reading public was, and would continue to be, self-subverting. Michael Anesko explains that while new opportunities were made available by marketplace growth, the "conditions by which such phenomenal growth was achieved carried with them new threats to the writer's integrity and to the very habits

---

[4] James Hepburn, *The Author's Empty Purse & the Rise of the Literary Agent* (London: Oxford UP, 1968) 24.

[5] Mary Ann Gillies, *The Professional Literary Agent in Britain: 1880-1920* (Toronto: U of Toronto P, 2007) 35.

of mind that made possible the creations of a lasting and significant literature."[6] That integrity and the habits of many of Pinker's clients would make this particular agent's job during the remainder of his life quite difficult, as his work for James, detailed herein, demonstrates.

The last decade of the nineteenth century marked a series of endings for James on a personal and professional level. The author struggled with the loss of family and close friends to illness and possibly suicide, coupled with experiments in the theatre that began well but ended miserably. In true Jamesian fashion, he made use of his experiences by translating them into modifications of his craft, which changed markedly by the turn of the century. Just as his writing changed, so did the opportunities by which he might place it.

The International Copyright Act of 1891, or Chace Act, which offered legal protection to authors who wished to publish in the United States and foreign countries as long as those authors deposited a copy of their work (a copy printed in the United States, not manufactured in a foreign country) to the Library of Congress before or on the day of publication in the other country, came far too late to protect the American rights to the wildly popular and financially successful pirated *Daisy Miller* more than a decade earlier, but created possibilities that took time to investigate and negotiate, time that James held dear to his craft.[7]

In February 1888 he wrote his brother William that he had hired an agent who "appeared eager to undertake *me*" who will take ten percent while taking "favorable action on one's market" and offered "relief & comfort of having him take all the mercenary & *selling* side off one's

---

[6] Michael Anesko, *Friction With the Market: Henry James and the Profession of Authorship* (New York, Oxford UP, 1986) 34.

[7] The United States Copyright Act of 1909 was the only other copyright law that would have affected James during his lifetime, providing for double the copyright length from 28 to 56 years. This was not an issue for either the author or Pinker.

mind," noting as well that the agent could be "terminated at any moment if they don't do."[8]

Alexander, or A.P., Watt, who is widely considered the first professional literary agent, became successful by aligning himself with authors who were proven financial successes themselves as well as by working with publishers to his advantage. He "functioned as a middleman between writers and publishers, and he flourished partly because he kept the interests of the publishers in mind when he negotiated."[9] James may have turned to Watt when the unthinkable happened; the *Atlantic* refused his short story "The Pupil." James, however, had approached Watt through the agent's client Walter Besant before this "shock of a perfectly honest surprise."[10]

James was particularly upset because the *Atlantic* had published his first signed fiction, "The Story of a Year," in March 1865 and had consistently accepted his short stories, reviews, and essays since then. This refusal may be explained by the reduction in commercial value of James's work, reflected also in the advance offered by Frederick Macmillan for *The Tragic Muse*, which put James on edge in his negotiations with the publisher on March 26, 1890: "I'm afraid I can't meet you on the ground of your offer in regard to the publication of 'The Tragic Muse' in this country [England] - two thirds in the future. That future is practically remote & I am much concerned with the present"[11] and again, two days later: "Unless I can put the matter on a

---

[8] Philip Horne, Ed. *Henry James: A Life in Letters* (London: Allen Lane, 1999) 200.

[9] James L. W. West III, *American Authors and the Literary Marketplace Since 1900* (Philadelphia: U of Pennsylvania P, 1988) 78.

[10] Henry James to Horace Scudder, editor of the *Atlantic*, 10 November 1890. Rpt. in George Monteiro, "The Atlantic Monthly's Rejection of 'The Pupil': An Exchange of Letters Between Henry James and Horace Scudder," *American Literary Realism, 1870-1910* 23 (Fall 1990): 75-83. 79.

[11] Horne, *Henry James: A Life* 219.

more remunerative footing all round I shall give up my English 'market'
- heaven save the market! & confine myself to my American."[12]

James mentions that he is aware that his last books haven't sold to
Macmillan's advantage and that is actually in debt to them; but he still
needs more money for the new book. Less than a week later, Watt
proved useful in arranging a more acceptable financial settlement (£250
for British and colonial rights for five years and two months) with
the same publisher: "I hear with pleasure from you that you have so
promptly arranged the matter of *The Tragic Muse*: I am quite content
with the result."[13]

James met and befriended young Wolcott Balestier, an American
author who worked for the New York publisher John W. Lovell
and eventually collaborated with Heinemann to publish English and
American work on the continent, as he wrote to William Dean Howells
in May 1890: "I have lately seen much the admirably acute & intelligent
young Balestier, who has been of much business use to me & a great
comfort thereby - besides my liking him so. I think that practically
he will soon 'do everything' for me."[14] Balestier negotiated terms with
Edward Compton for the production of the theatrical version of *The
American*, which James had adapted during the fall of 1890, by the
Compton Comedy Company in England. This collaboration between
author and producer was successful, as James wrote to George du
Maurier in January of the following year: "We really did very well
indeed."[15] Reviews ranged from claims that "James is at the height of
his fame as a novelist" and promised "no small enrichment of the stage

---

[12] Ibid. 220.

[13] Ibid. 221.

[14] Ibid. 224.

[15] Ibid. 237.

with his "evident theatrical talent"[16] to those of Harriet W. Preston, who called the first act "tiresome and irrelevant" with characters who were "colorless and overacted."[17] James seemed affected more by the popular and immediate response than the written reviews and was pleased by the apparent acceptance. Unfortunately, the partnership between James and Balestier ended tragically when the younger man died in Dresden of typhoid in December 1891.

A series of deaths surrounded that of Balestier, including those of James's old friend James Russell Lowell in August 1891 and six months later his sister Alice: "It makes a great difference in my life - but I must live with the difference as long as I live at all,"[18] he wrote Elizabeth Lewis five days after Alice's death. Meanwhile, *The American* was still holding its own on the road and James continued to work on both drama and fiction in spite of his personal losses. Close friend and valuable source of gossip and social information Fanny Kemble died in 1893 as James focused on polishing the play *Guy Domville*, the successor to *The American*.

The following year proved doubly tragic with the surprising suspected suicide of Constance Fenimore Woolson, who often shared quarters with James as a traveling companion in Venice, and the death of Robert Louis Stevenson, who had inspired James with his fearlessness and thrilling writing: "that he's silent forever will be a fact hard, for a long time, to live with,"[19] he lamented to Edmund Gosse in December 1894. In spite of these troubles, between *The Tragic Muse* in 1890 and the

---

[16] Anon., "The News in London," *New York Tribune*, 11 January 1891, 1. Rpt. in Linda J. Taylor, *Henry James, 1866-1916, a Reference Guide* (Boston: G. K. Hall, 1982) 191.

[17] Harriet W. Preson, "Mr. James's 'American' on the London Stage," *Atlantic Monthly* 68 (December 1891): 846-848. Rpt. in Taylor, 191.

[18] Horne, *Henry James: A Life* 248.

[19] Ibid. 271.

beginning of 1895 he managed to find time and motivation to assemble and negotiate terms for the publication of three short story collections, two volumes of essays, and four plays.

The year 1895, however, promised a turn in fortunes professionally that must have encouraged James as he managed emotional upheaval as continued personal tragedies darkened the decade. The play he had finished for Compton over a year before, *Guy Domville*, was scheduled for production in London on January 5, and for James there was no reason to think that it would be any less successful than his adaptation of *The American* four years earlier, which had enjoyed popular if not critical success for over two years. Unfortunately, it was not to be.

After an opening night that closed with a confusing blur of catcalls and applause when James took the stage, *Guy Domville* lasted only one month with 39 performances (earning the author $1300), suffering the opposite fate of its predecessor; critical acceptance and popular failure. James's distress at this response was only magnified by his earlier reaction to *The American*: "James turned to the theater in the hope, not only of money, but of a tangible response to his work. The extreme elation at Southport [*The American*] would be the result, literally, of the physical conditions of the theatre: a visible audience, audible applause."[20]

One anonymous reviewer referred to *Domville* as "a stupendous failure"[21] but well-known London critic William Archer praised the play while criticizing the audience's behavior.[22] Decades later, Leon Edel would speculate that "the fundamental truth was that he was too

---

[20] Roger Gard, *Henry James: The Critical Heritage* (New York: Barnes & Noble, 1968) 13.

[21] Anon., "Henry James's Play Fails," *New York Times*, 6 January 1895, 5. Rpt in Taylor, 225.

[22] Anon., "Henry James's Play," *New York Times*, 27 January 1895, 14. Rpt. in Taylor, 189.

refined and subtle a talent to reach the 'common man.'"[23] James, as always, seemed to focus on the negative responses and complained to Howells: "I'm utterly out of it here - & Scribner, the Century, the Cosmopolitan, will have nothing to say to me - above all for fiction. The *Atlantic* & H&M [Houghton Mifflin] treat me like the dust beneath their feet, the Macmillans, here, have cold-shouldered me out of all relation with them."[24]

James's embarrassment and disappointment were acute, but not such that his devotion to his work was stunted. He rededicated his efforts to fiction while lamenting his failure in the theater, publishing yet another volume of short stories by the end of the year and making use of his experience writing drama to set a more effective stage, so to speak, for his new work: "he would never again write the kind of novel he had written before his dramatic years. The stage had given him new technical skills; these he would now use in his fiction."[25]

His concerns for his declining income kept him working as well; he was used to a comfortable amount to support his extravagant lifestyle without using his inheritance and worried that the less than $2500 per year he was averaging would not be substantial enough.[26] As Matthiessen remarks of the notebook begun during this year, it "illustrates the fertility of his middle years; it contains

---

[23] Leon Edel, *The Life of Henry James: The Treacherous Years, 1895-1901* (New York: Lippincott, 1969) 91.

[24] Horne, *Henry James: A Life* 277-278.

[25] Edel, *The Treacherous Years* 111.

[26] Relative worth of the monetary values quoted herein can be calculated at http://ww w.measuringworth.com, where James's earning for *Guy Domville* ($1300 in 1895) translates into a compensation value in 2023 of $245,505; the "less than $2500" into $472,125. His financial concerns, which appear to revolve around social appearance and a sort of 'keeping up with the Joneses' (or Wharton née Jones) may be put into a better perspective with these figures.

the extensive development of *The Spoils of Poynton* and *What Maisie Knew,* the substantial nurturing of the 'germ' of *The Ambassadors,* and the marshaling of sundry ideas into manageable lists."[27]

While he completed *The Other House* and another short story collection, James decided that life in London, his primary residence of twenty years, had become counterproductive. The continuous movement, the social demands, and the closeness of others in general all made it difficult for him to write. He took a vacation to Rye on the southwest coast in 1896 and discovered a retreat suited to his artistic temperament, where he had peace and privacy along with room to bicycle in solitude. Unfortunately, his rest was disrupted by the death of old friend George du Maurier in October. He began dictating his work during the winter of 1896-1897 in the midst of *What Maisie Knew* after a summer struggling with writer's cramp, employing the very detailed and experienced stenographer William MacAlpine for the job.

James enjoyed the professional advice and assistance of William Dean Howells, his longtime mentor and friend, in the matter of placing the rather unorthodox *The Awkward Age* in 1897: "I am sure you will be glad to know what your magic voice has wrought - a proposal, on Nelson's part, to which I have already lucidly responded . . . you were wholly right as to the fee or guerdon - £600 is exactly what would have been the form of *my* golden dream, and is what I have directly named."[28] According to Fred Kaplan, this amount was unexpectedly high and undoubtedly due to Howells's influence with Henry Loomis Nelson, editor of *Harper's Weekly.*[29]

---

[27] F.O. Matthiessen and Kenneth B. Murdoch, Eds., *The Notebooks of Henry James* (New York: Oxford UP, 1955) 129.

[28] Michael Anesko, *Letters, Fictions, Lives: Henry James and William Dean Howells* (New York: Oxford UP, 1997) 304. Howells's response is not extant.

[29] Fred Kaplan, *Henry James: The Imagination of Genius: a Biography* (Baltimore: Johns Hopkins UP, 1999) 464.

James's relationship with Watt had ended some time before and while James was an old hand at pressing publishers for the financial value he attached to his work, Howells noted the difficulties his friend was having with the American market in particular.[30] While there is no documentation as to reasons for James to dismiss Watt, one can speculate that the particular agent's methods of working both sides of the literary fence, attempting to please both author and publisher, were not to James's liking or benefit. As Gillies puts it, "because Watt was slow to change, his rivals provided an important emerging coterie of authors and publishers."[31]

After James signed a twenty-one year lease on Lamb House, an idyllic property in Rye, in 1897, the financial burden of such a long commitment and the price of upkeep

created some distress, so James accepted an offer from Blackwood to compose a biography of William Wetmore Story (1903), a project that would haunt him for years because of a lack of material and a fear of displeasing members of Story's family. Edel notes that James, "in an era of copyright chaos, before the advent of the literary agent, negotiated and published in three literary capitals: Boston, New York and London. He bargained stiffly: he demanded his price and usually received it,"[32] but those days were over, and the author was reduced to accepting work that he would have, in the past, refused. Howells urged him to find another agent, and by the spring of the following year James had enlisted the aid of James Brand Pinker, former assistant editor of *Black and White*, a weekly to which the author contributed three stories from

---

[30] Anesko's handling of the James-Howells correspondence deals with these issues, as does his study of James's difficulties with the market forces in *Friction With the Market*.

[31] Gillies 38-39.

[32] Leon Edel and Dan Laurence, *A Bibliography of Henry James* 2nd Ed. (London: Hart-Davis, 1961) 12.

1891-1892.[33]

J.B., as he was known, had been in business as an agent for only two years before James approached him, but he was quite busy from the start of his enterprise. In 1895 he left his position as editor of *Pearson's Magazine* and in January 1896 he wrote to H.G. Wells offering his services as a literary agent. One of Pinker's first clients, Wells was a problematic one because of his habit of placing his work rather wildly prior to Pinker's intervention. This issue foreshadowed a problem Pinker would have with James, although James's was of a greater magnitude. Within his first couple of years as a literary agent, he managed to upset Oscar Wilde, who complained that Pinker "is not to be trusted" because the agent was unable to place *The Ballad of Reading Gaol* in 1897, and called Pinker "ridiculous" as well as an "absurdity."[34] In Pinker's defense, Josephine Guy and Ian Small explain that "Wilde's dismissal of Pinker is almost certainly unfair . . . Pinker had a reputation for succeeding with difficult writers, and his failure to place Wilde's work should perhaps be read less a testimony to his - that is, Pinker's - inadequacies than to the enormous difficulties posed by Wilde's reputation."[35]

Pinker's decision to work with and for an author was a commitment to labor tirelessly on behalf of that author, regardless of historical difficulties such as those Wells and Wilde brought to the table, without concern for the publishers involved, a claim that his competitor Watt was unable to make. Pinker would not accept a client in whom he did not believe and had an eye for talent that was a result of his days as

---

[33] "Sir Edmund Orme" 25 November 1891, "The Real Thing" 16 April 1892 and "The Visit" 28 May 1892.

[34] Merlin Holland and Rupert Hart-Davis, Eds. *The Complete Letters of Oscar Wilde* (London: Fourth Estate, 2000) 970, 972.

[35] Josephine M. Guy and Ian Small, *Oscar Wilde's Profession: Writing and the Culture Industry in the Late Nineteenth Century* (Oxford: Oxford UP 2000) 191.

a reader and an editor. His efforts went beyond financial reward; he wanted the work of his authors recognized for the genius he believed it to be. The personal financial stability gained upon his marriage to Mary Elizabeth Seabrooke, who brought money from her father's successful brewing business into the arrangement years earlier made these convictions possible.

He claimed to serve one master; his first and only allegiance was always to his author. By agreeing to represent an author, he made a statement of personal belief in the creative and financial possibilities of that author, and as such, was very discerning about choosing his clients, refusing material he felt he could not honestly represent. He was candid and aggressive, qualities that made some publishers uncomfortable and sometimes angry.

Pinker's careful handling of his authors show his concern for the sanctity of their craft and profession, and while he sometimes suggested revision or questioned suitability (only for authors who were agreeable to such advice; James definitely was not one), unlike Watt he did not believe that his job allowed him to advise authors as to the content of their work ("write what you want to write and don't worry. I'll sell it"[36]). He offered practical encouragement, personal instruction, and peace of mind in his efforts to foster his clients' literary production. Several scholars have looked closely at Pinker's relationship with Conrad in particular, including Frederick Karl, who calls the series of over 1200 letters between the agent and author Conrad's "true autobiography," and J.H. Stape and Owen Knowles, who, along with Keith Carabine, detail the troubles between the agent and Conrad during the composition of *Under Western Eyes* from 1908-1910; Stape and Knowles note the assistance of John Galsworthy, another Pinker client and friend of Conrad, who attempted to salvage the relationship during this stressful

---

[36] The *Bookman* (May 1922) 274.

period.

James Hepburn, editor of the letters of Arnold Bennett, details the relationship between Pinker and his most profitable client, as revealed through their correspondence, and Mary Ann Gillies, while focusing on Conrad's well-documented (by that time) relationship with the agent, also gives attention to Pinker's friendship with and work for Violet Martin and Edith Somerville, who published under the name Somerville and Ross. Pinker's partnership with James, his "close friend" and the first author noted in his obituary, has yet to be addressed to any depth, and while Rayburn Moore claims that "in the final analysis, James B. Pinker remains a background figure in James's circle"[37] in response to Alan Donovan's assertion in 1961 that "the most enlightening part of the Pinker letters [with respect to James] is the exact business relationship between author and agent which they delineate. It is in this most vital area that much profitable work remains to be done,"[38] Pinker's correspondence reveals that Moore could not be more mistaken.

Pinker's ability to deal diplomatically with difficult writers with delicate constitutions (of one sort or another) was, according to observers like Frank Swinnerton, very different from his attitude towards publishers: "He drove a hard bargain. I have seen magazine editors glower at him, and a publisher grew pale under his deadly silences."[39] His persuasive methods varied as necessary and his experience as an editor, reader, and journalist all contributed to knowledge of the publishing world that gave him and his clients in turn, an advantage the authors alone would not have had. He was an

---

[37] Moore, Rayburn S. "Henry James and 'The Pinker of Agents,' James B. Pinker." *PostSript: The Publication of the Philological Association of the Carolinas* 9 (1992): 89.

[38] Donovan, Alan B. "My Dear Pinker: The Correspondence of Henry James with His Literary Agent." *Library Gazette* 36 (1961): 88.

[39] Frank Swinnerton, *Background With Chorus* (London: Hutchinson, 1956) 129.

author's agent, as he was proud to say, and his allegiance was, without question, to his writers.

Pinker added George Gissing to his client list in 1898 along with Stephen Crane, and continued to push for the best terms for Wells. He frustrated publisher William Heinemann with his hard bargaining over *The War of the Worlds*, which makes Frederic Whyte's assertion that it was actually Heinemann, a notorious foe of literary agents, who gave his approval of and even possibly the idea for James to employ Pinker, amusing as well as inaccurate.[40] Unfortunately for Pinker, Heinemann was not alone in his distrust of agents. While Pinker wrestled with difficult authors, many of whom were friends of James, and stubborn publishers, James, as Ford Madox Ford dramatized, "had had financial misfortunes and the future looked like a gloomy vista of pinched discomfort. 'And then suddenly,' said Mr. James, 'along came a little man called . . . Pinker.' Pinker . . . jumped about and kept his promises. And all was gas and gingerbread."[41] Gingerbread aside, James's real and pressing need for a sense of financial stability in the face of an older home in need of repair and a longstanding commitment to a lifestyle that required a large and consistent income drew him to Pinker's doorstep, where he sent three stories in May and June of 1898.[42]

These three stories were like pebbles on a pond, rippling into an eighteen year partnership that moved from extreme highs to extreme lows on professional and personal levels, taking Pinker on a journey he accepted with the knowledge that James was past his popular prime. He

---

[40] "It was with complete approval, if not actually at his suggestion, that Mr. Pinker in 1898 became Henry James's agent." Frederic Whyte, *William Heinemann, A Memoir* (Garden City, NY: Doubleday Doran, 1929) 125.

[41] Ford Madox Ford, *Return to Yesterday* (New York: Liveright, 1932) 65.

[42] "The Great Condition," "The Given Case," and "The Great Good Place."

could not have been unaware of the author's reputation as a difficult, self-centered, and demanding man, but accepted the responsibility for promoting his work regardless, so that ultimately, his work as James's literary agent would be to preserve and promote the production of a genius.

Anesko notes that "what distinguishes James's career and gives it such documentary significance is the fact that he was among the first men of letters to deal effectively with publishers in both England and America."[43] By stepping into the picture at this time, Pinker accepted James's previous establishment of his own work on a transatlantic scale and accepted responsibility to promote it to publishers successfully regardless of the business problems the author had unknowingly created while managing his own work. The agent did this without any desire to modify the work James produced in order to suit the market or the publishers' needs; he never suggested the author alter the material in any creative way but agreed, rather, to sell what the author gave him as it stood.

Pinker's involvement in the production and marketing of James's work, placed in the context of James's career, changing literary and market conventions (including increased opportunities for promotion and profit, along with an expanding readership), criticism, and publishing history, was clearly vital to the continuance of James's literary career, as his later works and the New York Edition proved difficult material to manage and place. The agent's role as the mediator of conflict between the commercial writer and literary artist, positions that James had difficulty reconciling, had considerable influence on the shape of James's later career and thus the way in which the author and his work are remembered, which proves that James's legacy is clearly tied to Pinker's efforts.

---

[43] Anesko, *Friction* 36.

John O'London in the *New York Times* marked Pinker's ability to "bet on the side of literature"[44] when taking a chance on a new client; his 'bet' on James would give the author a new lease on his career as his writing method and product evolved. Using correspondence between Pinker, James, and the primary publishers of James's material from 1898 until Pinker's death in 1922, along with secondary works addressing the agent's endeavors and the general atmosphere of the publishing world during this period, *An Eye for Genius* demonstrates the necessary link between Pinker's work and James's continued presence before the public, both during his lifetime and after the author's death.

The agent's communications with publishers testifies to his dedication to serving his author in all efforts; he never lost sight of what he believed were James's best interests in spite of pressure from publishers during the twenty-four years he handled the author and his work. While Anesko believes that James's "behavior in the marketplace effectively demonstrates the changing nature of the literary vocation,"[45] it is truly Pinker who managed to keep James afloat during these changes while the author struggled with them on his own.

At this point during James's career the author recognized his inability to manage these changes and successfully chose the agent who would prove the best able to handle him as an artist and his work as a product of value in the literary marketplace, one who provided a business service personalized to the author's temperament and work habits as well as James's often unreasonable financial requirements and his need to maintain a presence before the reading public. As his friend Howells's consummate 'man of letters,' James could not reconcile his art with his need for popular and financial success; Pinker's intervention would allow the author to write the material he wished to write rather than

---

[44] John O'London, "London Book Talk" *New York Times* (5 March 1922): 58.

[45] Anesko, *Friction* 33.

what the current reading audience wanted, allowing him to remain an artist rather than attempt the role of businessman that would interfere with both his self-image as an artist and the time he took to write the lengthy and detailed work he produced.

Heinemann and Methuen

When James Brand Pinker stepped into his role as Henry James's literary agent in 1898, he found English publisher William Heinemann less than welcoming, as the two had recently battled over the financial terms for H. G. Wells's *The War of the Worlds*, so he worked towards establishing better terms for his new client with another English publisher, A.M.S. Methuen. James had been on friendly terms with Heinemann, an associate of Wolcott Balestier, for several years before deciding to publish with his firm. In 1894 the author praised him for his business expertise, noting that "everything you touch turns into gold,"[46] referring to Heinemann's first novel, Hall Caine's *The Bondsman*, which sold nearly half a million copies when it was published in 1890, and in 1895, James left his longtime English publisher, Macmillan, in a quest for a portion of that gold.

Macmillan, who had published James's first novel, *Roderick Hudson*, in 1879 and had continued to publish his work in England steadily since, had reduced what James considered an already small advance (£250 for *The Tragic Muse*, negotiated from an initial offer of £70) and James felt no reason to comply with the general trade courtesy of the time, that of allowing one's first publisher the opportunity to issue one's

---

[46] Henry James to William Heinemann, 2 November 1894. Rpt. in *Hound and Horn* 7 (Apr/June 1934): 415

subsequent material. Heinemann was no stranger to James's work; he had privately printed twenty copies of *The American: A Comedy in Four Acts* at the author's expense in September 1891. In 1895 he issued James's *Terminations* and the following year *Embarrassments*, both small collections of short stories.

James's next five titles were published in English editions by Heinemann: *The Other House* (1896 and 1897), *The Spoils of Poynton* (1897), *What Maisie Knew* (1897, also published as a serial in Heinemann's periodical *The New Review* from February to September that same year), *The Two Magics* (short story collection, 1898), and *The Awkward Age* (1899). Their relationship began to deteriorate in 1898, the same year James employed Pinker, and while Whyte suggests that "it was more from incompatibility of temperament than from any other cause that they drifted apart after the production of The Spoils of Poynton,"[47] John St. John, in his biography of the publisher, claims that James's "hopes for better rewards"[48] with Heinemann went unrealized.

According to James, however, Heinemann had let him know that he did not approve of the use of literary agents and the two had a "lively row" on the subject, which James described to his friend Lucy Clifford in a letter dated January 24, 1900[49]. James explained the problem to Pinker that same month, barely containing his amusement as he reassured the agent that he valued Pinker's services more than his relationship with Heinemann: "I have written to him repeating that I have placed the disposal of the book in question definitely in your hands & that it must

---

[47] Whyte 135.

[48] John St. John, *William Heinemann: A Century of Publishing, 1890-1990.* (London: Heinemann, 1990) 68.

[49] Leon Edel, Ed., *Henry James, Letters: 1895-1916.* (Cambridge: Harvard Up, 1984) 129-130.

remain in them. *That* point is therefore settled."[50]

Heinemann's aversion to agents had its roots in his belief that A.P Watt had ruined his opportunity to publish Rudyard Kipling, so he now refused to deal with them on principle. In 1904, Heinemann publicly accused Pinker of "unethical behavior and deliberate impoverishment"[51] of Joseph Conrad, who actually used Pinker as a personal banker as much as a negotiator of his literary interests. Keith Carabine states that along with dealing with "fussy insensitive publishers like Methuen," Pinker arranged for the typing of Conrad's work, lent him money for a variety of personal emergencies (rent, cigars, milk, income taxes, and a coat for his wife Jessie, who claimed that Pinker was a "delightful companion") and "listened to his endless self-justifications and laments about his own and his family's sundry sicknesses."[52]

Heinemann's distrust of agents and Pinker in particular did not prevent him from publishing Stephen Crane and Conrad, both Pinker clients, who, like James, were financial gambles, while capitalizing on popular Irish romantic novelist Margaret Hungerford's death by reprinting five of her bestselling books in 1902, which would have insured him against any loss on the work of the three more literary authors.[53] He continued, however, to refuse to deal through Pinker, insisting on contacting James directly instead, and expressed an interest in James's travel writings, maintaining a deferential approach to the author up through the years leading to his death.

Pinker, undaunted by Heinemann's disdain, began working with

---

[50] Horne, *Henry James: A Life* 334.

[51] David Finkelstein, "James Brand Pinker," *Oxford Dictionary of National Biography*, Ed. H.C.G. Matthew and Brian Harrison, Vol. 44. (Oxford: Oxford UP, 2004) 148.

[52] Keith Carabine, "Conrad, Pinker, and Under Western Eyes: A Novel," *Conradian* 10 (1985): 145.

[53] Whyte notes that Heinemann published James "doubtless, much more for the honour of the thing than with any hope of considerable financial reward." 128.

Methuen at the turn of the century to establish James's works in the English market for the best possible price, regardless of the author's previous long standing relationship with Macmillan as well as the current one with Heinemann. During this time, Methuen was publishing Wells's science fiction and fantasy tales and later, in 1908, Oscar Wilde's collected works. Both authors were Pinker clients, and the agent most certainly used his established connection through Wells to help with the James negotiations.

Methuen was a choice publisher from a financial standpoint, as he offered a higher royalty rate than other publishers, beginning with the standard ten percent and increasing to twelve and a half after the first 500 copies sold. Pinker could not have known, even with James's prolific history, that with James he was beginning a management endeavor that would entrust him with over 3000 pages of writing over the next four years, or what Robert Gale calls "the most impressive stage of writing . . . in the annals of American literary history."[54] The agent was just as busy as James.

Methuen wrote Pinker in January 1900 confirming an agreement for English and colonial rights to a short story collection (not yet called *The Soft Side*) with an advance of £100. The £100 is crossed out and replaced with a handwritten £150, presumably by Pinker, who was always, at James's instruction, out for the 'down.' The following day, James penned an approval of Pinker's work to the agent, claiming that the arrangements were "highly satisfactory" and asking for an early publication date, noting that he would be writing to George Brett at the American Macmillan's, who would offer at least the same.[55] Pinker doesn't seem to have been bothered by the author's handling of

---

[54] Robert L. Gale, "Henry James." *Dictionary of Literary Biography: American Realists and Naturalists* (Detroit: Gale, 1982) 315.

[55] Horne, *Henry James: A Life* 334-335.

negotiations when James saw fit to enter the fray, but took up the reins when James began and left the finalization to Pinker. Pinker would, then and in the future, take the industry standard ten percent from James's advances and royalties as payment for his services, regardless of any work James (or anyone else) did on his own behalf when the urge struck or when James was contacted directly by editors or publishers.

Methuen had no trouble working with Pinker in any regard and approached him for all manner of concerns. Just over a week after sending a portion of the advance he wrote: "in the first place, cannot you get Henry James to hit upon a general title for his stories."[56] Pinning James down for a title for marketing purposes would be the least of Methuen's (and Pinker's) troubles as the year advanced. While James completed *The Sacred Fount*, his first novel written under the agent's care, Pinker found himself simultaneously working out the details of an agreement with Methuen and advocating for the English publisher in terms of dealing with the slow production of *The Soft Side* by the American Macmillans.

Adding to the complications, in July 1900 James declared (quite rightly) that *The Sacred Fount* was not fit for serialization, focusing on its financial possibilities rather than his reasons for thinking so, and asked for any sum "down" that was "respectable."[57] As always, the 'down' was his primary concern. James recognized that the political climate (the Second Boer War)[58] was making the agent's job more difficult, noting that "I hope you bear up - though I'm afraid 'trade' doesn't - under

---

[56] A.M.S. Methuen to James B. Pinker, 7 February 1900, Henry James Collection, Yale Collection of American Literature, Beinecke Rare Book and Manuscript Library, New Haven, Connecticut.

[57] Edel, *Henry James: Selected Letters* 321.

[58] Incidentally, the War brought a different sort of material to place to Pinker's attention. The death of reporter G.W. Steevens from typhoid left the matter of the publication of the correspondent's letters, which Pinker arranged with *Blackwood's* for £700.

this temperature, and everything else,"[59] but still made his financial expectations clear. Pinker did not disappoint.

Two days from the date of James's letter, Methuen wrote Pinker to make his interest in the novel known, which only could have come about through Pinker's machinations prior to the author's instruction. Twelve days later, the publisher sent a signed copy of the agreement for *The Sacred Fount*, followed by a check for £150 less than a week after. In between the formalities Pinker was managing, James wrote to his friend William Dean Howells to explain that the novel was not to be serialized but clarified that it was through the fault of the work itself ("it is indeed inapt"[60]) absolving by such claim the efforts, or any implied lack thereof, of his agent.

While finalizing terms for the book, Pinker was also dealing with the death of Stephen Crane and his grasping 'widow,' Cora. He warned James and other Crane friends and acquaintances that Cora was soliciting money and should be turned away, as Wells had already been quite generous with her. Pinker had spent the better part of the previous two years providing the Cranes with funds for their rent and other necessities, including the wine dealer's bill. While Wells assisted Cora, Pinker helped Wells handle the construction of Wells's new home, including managing the negotiations between the solicitor and the architect, seeing even to the storage of the family's furniture, details that were too stressful for the author to deal with while attempting to produce material for the agent to sell.

Wells seems to have forgotten this extraordinary assistance, which was decidedly above and beyond the usual duties of a literary agent, when he chided Pinker only a few years later, claiming that "in the last three or four years you have not relieved me of any anxiety or saved

---

[59] Ibid. 321.

[60] Horne, *Henry James: A Life* 338.

me from several losses."[61] Fifteen years later, Wells, shifting moods, would advise James Joyce to employ Pinker, who would go on to handle negotiations for *Portrait of the Artist as a Young Man* and *Ulysses*, although his death in 1922 would prevent him from seeing the latter in print.[62]

In the midst of the flurry of contracts and drama, Pinker received a letter from James MacArthur of Doubleday dated August 28, 1900, the publication date of *The Soft Side*, to refuse the same, which Pinker had submitted to him in June that year at James's suggestion. MacArthur refers to the "peculiar terms"[63] Pinker had proposed, which speaks to the uncommon nature of James's financial requirements and the agent's undaunted desire to meet them. Ultimately in this case he was successful, as he had obviously not waited for the Doubleday response but moved forward to place the book where he could on satisfactory terms. Satisfactory for James, that is.

Methuen, unaware that Pinker had been playing the field, wrote to the agent in October to complain about the various publishers involved in the production of James's material, referring to them as "Hy James' flittings."[64] Four days later, he wrote again, asking if James would like to make arrangements for Methuen to publish a long novel, two years hence, and if it "deal with its motive in a manner not too recondite we would pay him the sum of £300 on account of the usual royalties."[65]

While the long novel published in the fall of 1902 would be *The Wings of the Dove*, sold to English publisher Archibald Constable and offered, only days before Methuen's October request, to Charles Scribner's Sons

---

[61] Norman and Jeanne Mackenzie, *H.G. Wells: A Biography* (New York: Simon, 1973) 187.

[62] Joyce refers to the agent in the *Circe* chapter of *Ulysses*

[63] Letters Sent to James B. Pinker Concerning Henry James

[64] Ibid.

[65] Ibid.

in America, the equally 'recondite' one suggested by Methuen would become *The Ambassadors.* The author's 'flittings' clearly did not alter the publisher's interest in his work, as frustrating as it must have been to wait for information from James through Pinker and deal with the machinations between the pair and other publishers. Handling all of James's material would have been a pipe dream for any publisher; a dream that might have become a nightmare if it had ever come true.

At the beginning of October 1900, which was proving a busy month for correspondence, James wrote to his sister-in-law Alice James to express his pleasure with his agent's work: "the excellently effective Pinker is bringing me up & round, so promisingly that it really contains the germs of a New Career."[66] Pinker had shielded the author from the business end of troubles, leaving him to his craft without the stress of worrying about such trivialities as contracts and negotiations. After two years of professional association, the agent knew that James was counting on him to do his job completely in that regard, bothering him with such details only when absolutely necessary. Pinker was confident in his own abilities to deal with the difficulties brought about by James's inexplicable work habits and accepted that those habits would not change even if they were addressed as a problem; managing the work when and as given to him was Pinker's task as he continued to find complications along that path.

A few months after James's ringing endorsement, Pinker found a technicality while working on the contract for the American edition of *The Sacred Fount* that would prove an ongoing problem with Scribner and Methuen, one that had nothing to do with the author or his production practices. Pinker had to alter Scribner's initial contract for the book in January 1901 by deleting Scribner's Canadian rights because Methuen's Colonial Library edition included the same, and the contract

---

66 Horne, *Henry James: A Life* 345.

with Methuen had been signed and monies advanced nearly five months earlier. Pinker would find himself advocating for Methuen on this issue later in their relationship, attempting to prevent any problems with sales that might affect his author's earnings or the ease with which they could be determined and collected. As always, Pinker's bottom line would be James's cut, and he would do what was necessary to ensure the author received it as soon as possible without complications.

After a year of silence between Methuen and the James camp, presumably because of James's commitment to *The Wings of the Dove* for Constable and Scribner (detailed in the next chapter), the author agreed with Methuen through Pinker in March 1903 to supply two novels in 1904, *The Golden Bowl* (which James had started to write the previous summer) and *The Sense of the Past*, which was never completed but even in its partial form inspired a play and films after the author's death.

By August 1903 Methuen's concern was focused on *The Ambassadors*, spoken for back in 1900. He asked Pinker to help expedite the acquisition of the material, while James complained to his agent that Harper, the American publisher, was slow getting proof of the last third of the novel to him for corrections. James had given the finished manuscript to Pinker in July 1901 and it was forwarded to Harper, where it sat at an editor's desk for nearly two years. Pinker, in the middle of the two frustrated parties, circumvented the need for Harper's cooperation with Methuen's request by purchasing the *North American Review* (the Heinemann periodical that serialized the novel from January to December of 1903) issue of August 15, 1903. James would use the text to create copy to send to Methuen.

Less than two months later, James admitted to Pinker that he would be unable to complete *The Golden Bowl* for Methuen in November as promised. Pinker immediately addressed Methuen, resulting in an offer of extension to which James agreed in November, "with thanks, as on the whole it will ease me off and contribute to the higher perfection, so to speak, of the book."[67] He did not quite admit to the truth that it was really impossible for him to finish it at all while hammering out *The Ambassadors* under such awkward and high-pressure circumstances. James did complain just a bit, however, as "my only regret will be in having, alas, to wait so long for my money."[68] The author's concern for money, which was not expressed as a desire for his agent to request any specific sum, was obviously meant to convey that any such effort would be welcome.

James once again turned to Howells, writing in January 1904 to complain about the failure of *The Golden Bowl* to be published as a serial, as it isn't "alas, so employable - being contracted for, with Methuen here and Scribner's in New York, as a volume only, and on no brilliant terms."[69] His issue with the 'terms' seems invalid, as he as well as his agent had agreed to them.

By May 1904, James seemed to have conveniently forgotten his role in the delay of *The Golden Bowl* and began to complain to Pinker: "Methuen's importunity does meanwhile, I confess, distress me."[70] The publisher, meanwhile, was depending on corrected proofs from Scribner's to set up his English edition. Pinker, knowing full well that James was to blame for the initial delay, played along and did not remind the author of his role in the difficulties. In September 1904 James reminded Scribner that he needed "duplicates. I depend on them for Methuen & Co."[71] Scribner's wanted simultaneous publication with the English edition and as James was traveling in America to gather

---

[67] Ibid. 385.

[68] Ibid. 385.

[69] Ibid. 395.

[70] Ibid. 400.

[71] Ibid. 404.

material for a series of essays on his homeland, the opportunity to capitalize on his visit by publishing while he was present.

Methuen refused to name a publication date before seeing the length of the book and determining how much time it would take to print. In an effort to accommodate both parties and bring his client closer to remuneration, Pinker wrote to Scribner's at the end of September asking that six copies of the book be sent to Methuen; the author sent proofs to Methuen of his own accord less than two weeks later. In October, George Webster at Methuen replied politely but firmly that "it would not be possible for us to publish the book this year, and as it is a very long work we shall in all probability be unable to get copies ready in time to make simultaneous publication with America." He noted that James had not told him when publication was to be made in America, and suggested that Scribner send copies of the American edition to use as formal publication in England and maintain simultaneous publication as requested by Scribner's. He ended as he began, removing all blame from his house: "Trusting that the above arrangement will appear to you to be the best way of getting out of a difficulty which I do not think we can be held responsible for."[72]

Methuen himself wrote Pinker two days after Webster, indicating that he had been on holiday when Pinker sent him the September letter. Pinker's letter is unavailable, but one might guess from Methuen's response that it was insistent on financial matters, specifically an advance, without acknowledgement of James's part in the publication date difficulties: "I don't think we ought to pay Henry James' advance as the postponement is in no way due to us."[73] The publisher would have only just received the remainder of the manuscript and was nowhere near realizing any benefit from it, and yet, as Pinker would manage time

---

[72] Henry James Collection, Yale Collection of American Literature

[73] Ibid.

and again, the advance was expected regardless of standard publishing practice.

Methuen was willing to let the "question of principle" slide and offered £100, which must have met with Pinker's polite disdain. Less than a week later, the publisher wrote again, reiterating that the agent really was not playing fair "to ask us to pay anything to Henry James at present. . . it would be physically impossible to publish it even in five weeks from now." He offered £100 again, to be paid towards the end of November, and the remainder of the advance in January when he could actually publish the material. "I trust this will seem reasonable,"[74] he implored, but James weighed in with Pinker as to Methuen's "delay," his concern over a few months' wait for publication motivated, of course, by the accompanying delay in payment.

Methuen, by this point, was so distressed by the situation and the implication by James and Pinker that he was entirely at fault, although he had received the last of the manuscript less than two weeks earlier and Scribner had not yet produced the work for him to view, that he referred to the American publisher incorrectly in his pleading to Pinker at the end of October that "Messrs. Harper" (actual publisher, Scribner) needed to send copies to him so that simultaneous publication could take place. This slip may have been a fallback to similar issues Methuen had obtaining copy of *The Ambassadors* from Harper's over a year earlier.

The same day of this letter, he penned another to Pinker, a final surrender to the pressure as well as an acknowledgement that the agent was not the root of the problem: "Have you received from him [James] a definite and personal request for the money? If so, I shall be quite happy to do what is polite and agreeable." After a fairly consistent amount of bullying from Pinker's pen, he was willing to feed the beast but not quite without the last word: "I don't think a publisher should be asked to

---

[74] Ibid.

pay the advance on a book which he cannot possibly publish at present and that not through his own fault but through the fault of the author. This surely is a reasonable attitude. At the same time, there are always exceptions and I am always willing to be courteous."[75]

Pinker replied immediately upon receipt (October 26), presumably to acknowledge that indeed, the request was personal (wasn't it always?) and quite necessary, because Methuen sent a check for the offered £100 just as quickly (October 27), reiterating that the "remainder will be paid on the publication of the book early next year."[76] Pinker's incessant push for money to satisfy his client's financial concerns was finally successful, and at least Pinker could say that James was agreeable when it came time for proof corrections: there were none, which allowed Methuen to write "our printers to get to press without delay."[77] Scribner produced the American edition in November, but Methuen was unable to accomplish the same in England until February 1905. During that time period (1904-1905), Methuen was generally occupied with the publication of histories, biographies, and legal materials along with the occasional work of fiction, including G.K. Chesterton, Hilaire Belloc, Marie Corelli, Mrs. Hugh Fraser, and Mrs. C.N. Williamson, another Pinker client. The authors who accompanied James on the Methuen list were all rather successful investments by the publishing firm who would have made it possible for Methuen to take a financial chance on James, but definitely not with an advance arrangement without a full manuscript in hand, save for Pinker's aggressive encouragement.

Pinker revisited the earlier issue of copyright between Methuen and Scribner two days before the English edition was published, in Methuen's defense. Scribner had been supplying copies of the American

---

[75] Ibid.

[76] Ibid.

[77] Pinker, James B., Charles Deering McCormick Library of Special Collections.

edition of *The Golden Bowl* to booksellers on the continent, and Pinker wrote to Charles Scribner on February 8, 1905 asking him to "take measures to prevent this as it is of course interfering with the sale of their [Methuen] edition."[78] Six months later, A.P. Watt, representing Methuen, approached Scribner's on their continued practice in spite of Pinker's request: "We found to our dismay that when we published our edition the Parisian booksellers would not take our book because they said they had already been supplied from the United States."[79]

Pinker would find himself crossing out Canadian rights in Scribner's agreements (as he had for *The Golden Bowl*) as late as 1914, as the publisher kept trying to usurp Methuen's (and later, Dent's) established territory; while the Canadian rights were a part of Scribner's standard contract (continental rights were not, but that did not keep them from providing Paris shops with *The Golden Bowl*) they ignored Pinker's strikethroughs and went ahead, clearly preferring to wait for a reprimand before adhering, when forced, to the agent's request.

James, meanwhile, did not appreciate the trouble Methuen had taken regarding the issue of *The Golden Bowl* in such short order, in spite of the author's delay and the strong-arming of the advance, and complained to Wells in November 1905. His rather dramatic and emotional outpouring is worth quoting in full: "And let me just say just one word of attenuation of my (only apparent) meanness over the *Golden Bowl*. I was in America when that work appeared & it was published there in 2 vols & in very charming & readable form, each vol. but moderately thick & with a legible, handsome, large-typed page. But there came over to me a copy of the London issues, fat, vile, small-typed, horrific, prohibitive, that so broke my heart that I vowed I wouldn't, for very shame, disseminate it, & I haven't, with that feeling had a copy

---

[78] Archives of Charles Scribner's Sons.

[79] Ibid.

in the house or sent one to a single friend. I wish I had an American one at your disposition - but I have been again & again depleted of all ownership in respect to it. You are very welcome to the British brick if you, at this late day, will have it."[80]

The 'British brick,' Methuen's attempt to fit the greatly enlarged and frustratingly delayed novel into the originally planned one volume design, was nearly 600 pages "issued in drab blue linen-grain cloth" while the Scribner's edition was two volumes "issued in faded rose-sateen smooth cloth."[81] James's complaint was a clear refusal to take into account his own role in the delay, or the fact that the British editions were generally not the most attractive as a rule. He took the book's appearance as a personal slight (as he did so many things) rather than the result of his own work habits and the usual plain look of British editions. James had always been concerned about the physical appearance of his publications and often praised the productions as 'pretty' and 'charming,' complaining when the public didn't appreciate the books as if it was a slight to their physical beauty. Pinker's silent agreement with his client allowed James's denial of his involvement in any disagreeable aspect of publication, including the finished product as a material object, as well as his self-centered behavior (so antagonistic to publisher relations) to continue. Methuen, who obviously had been through a difficult time with James and Pinker, was questioned by members of his firm about his continued interest in the author, but *The Golden Bowl* was to be his reward, for it soon went into a second and third edition."[82]

James's focus for the next several years would be his collected edition

---

[80] Horne, *Henry James: A Life* 425.

[81] Edel, *Bibliography* 128.

[82] Maureen Duffy, *A Thousand Capricious Chances: A History of the Methuen List, 1889-1989.* (London: Methuen, 1989) 36. *The Golden Bowl* would become the best selling English edition of any James novel.

and travel writings, but in January 1910 Pinker approached Methuen regarding a collection of short stories (*The Finer Grain*) and the publisher responded positively: "we shall be happy to undertake the publication . . . on the terms you suggest."[83] By September, Methuen found the author still in the habit of running behind schedule, and had to write asking the agent for proof of the book, which was under contract to be published on October 6, 1910, as the publisher wanted review copies several days ahead of that date for marketing purposes. *The Finer Grain* was indeed published the next month, and the next year, Methuen undertook the publication of James's play *The Outcry*, issuing 2000 copies, most of which would only take up space in the publisher's warehouse and end up being sold at remainder prices.

In a letter to highly successful Pinker author Arnold Bennett (who had left A.P. Watt for Pinker) in March 1913, Methuen reflected on the nature of Pinker's methods over a decade after beginning his work with James and the agent: "Pinker is an excellent agent but I think that in this case he had been a little over earnest in watching over your interests."[84] The publisher most likely did not limit this opinion of the agent to his work for Bennett; surely the struggle with Pinker over James's production habits and insistence on money at non-traditional points in the publishing process were lodged in his memory. Pinker subsidized Bennett (the author referred to Pinker's "sweet reasonableness in finance") as he had Conrad, for nearly a decade, giving him money like an allowance on a monthly basis, and was most likely as fierce in his protection of Bennett's writing process and financial gains as he was with James's, although Bennett was a prodigious producer of material that sold well. Methuen maintained its professional standards

---

[83] James B. Pinker and Son: Collection of Papers, 1893-1940.

[84] Hepburn, James, Ed. *Letters of Arnold Bennett Volume 1: Letters to J.B. Pinker* (London: Oxford UP, 1966) 178.

when dealing with Pinker after James's death, and sent money to cover a percentage of the profit when they granted permission to another publisher to print *The Soft Side*, although the author was no longer living. The diligent Pinker would have taken his ten percent before adding the remainder to the James estate.

Pinker's manner of dealing with Methuen reflected his primary concern for James, regardless of how the publishers may have viewed his methods. Clearly James was at fault on more than one occasion for publication dates that interfered with his financial expectations but Pinker did not admonish him nor did he acknowledge the fact to Methuen, with whom he might have commiserated in confidence, but rather placed the publisher at a disadvantage under a barrage of consistent pressure to pay and print regardless of the practical problems created by the author's failure to adhere to promised delivery dates and further delays on the part of the American publishers Harper and Scribner.

Methuen remained interested in James's work in the midst of Pinker's heavy-handed approach. The publisher continued a professional relationship with the agent as the holders of several of James's copyrights and did benefit from Pinker's efforts to protect their Canadian interests. Any complications regarding copyrights could, of course, produce problems collecting royalties for his already anxious client, so Pinker's assistance to Methuen was tied absolutely to his interest in James. Collecting advances would be a strong point for the agent, as he successfully worked both Methuen and Scribner at the same time for money down on *The Golden Bowl*.

Constable, Houghton Mifflin, Macmillan, and Scribner

Although the house of Charles Scribner had published James's work, including his early novel *Confidence,* in its periodicals (*Scribner's Monthly* and *Scribner's Magazine*) for over 25 years before Pinker began representing the author, it was Pinker who managed James's first book publication with the American publisher. Editor Roger Burlingame mentions in his memoir that his father Edward "spotted" James in 1879, and wrote to Charles Scribner to encourage relations: "He is entirely *unattached* in the matter of publishing; and his future is certainly valuable enough to make an effort to connect him here."[85] Scribner's had a reputation for offering new authors, including Edith Wharton, Theodore Roosevelt, and George Santayana a start and maintaining career-length relationships with them.

James incorrectly valued his new agent's influence in a letter to William Dean Howells in September 1899: "It *may* come to pass that my 'literary agent,' though not of much use for anywhere but this country [England], shall find himself approaching the cold theatre of my early triumphs as a supplicant."[86] Less than a year later in July 1900, Pinker

---

[85] Roger Burlingame, *Of Making Many Books: A Hundred Years of Reading, Writing and Publishing* (New York: Scribner, 1946) 44.

[86] Anesko, *Letters* 353.

contacted Scribner's regarding *The Sacred Fount*, in fact on the very same day that he received the manuscript from the author, noting that James believed (quite correctly) that it was not fit as a serial and also that it would be "most convenient" to the author to have an arrangement "providing for the immediate payment for the book rights" to meet "his desire for immediate financial result."[87] Pinker asked for and received an advance of £400, acknowledging the receipt of the same as an opportunity to offer another novel in progress, only just sold in England to Archibald Constable on the same terms as *The Sacred Fount*.

In October 1900, Pinker approached Constable, the firm known for handling Walter Scott's material three-quarters of a century earlier and more recently, Bram Stoker's *Dracula*, regarding the work that would become *The Wings of the Dove*. That same month, the publisher sent a signed contract (terms unknown) to Pinker, calling for a delivery deadline of September 1, 1901. Scribner's made an offer that Pinker accepted in November for the same novel promised for the same date; at that point in time it was not only unnamed but unattended by the author. A year before offering *Wings* to Scribner's, Pinker received a letter from James in October 1899 announcing his work on a new novel, making the point that, as always, "it is highly important to me that a part of any such arrangement shall be for serial as well as book-rights."[88] The composition of *Wings* began, then, before that of *The Sacred Fount*, which was written and sold in 1900.

James explained to his agent in May 1900 that there would be a further delay in the completion of *Wings* because "Harper and Brothers have within the last fortnight asked me for a serial (not *that* one - a

---

[87] Archives of Charles Scribner's Sons.

[88] Stephanie Vincec, C.S.J., "'Poor Flopping Wings'": The Making of Henry James's *The Wings of the Dove.*" *Harvard Library Bulletin* 24 (1976): 65.

different and special thing:) and I have said a general Yes."[89] This 'special thing' would become *The Ambassadors*, and in the excitement of the opportunity to serialize this new project, *Wings* was set aside yet again, so by the time *Ambassadors* was complete in July 1901 and James returned to *Wings* it was clear that he would be unable to meet the original deadline of September. On the last day of June 1901 he wrote Pinker to ask him to request a postponement and a two month extension: "Will you kindly write to Scribner on the subject of the inevitable delay & my regrets at it."[90] The day after James penned this request, Pinker begged the publisher for "indulgence for Mr. Henry James"[91] as he would not have the work finished on time, noting that the author was working on another book for serialization, hence the delay. In James's defense, he did accept the terms for *The Ambassadors* before signing for *Wings* with Scribner's, but his time management skills were lacking in determining how much work he could handle at one time. Pinker most likely found it was not all that much trouble to 'beg indulgence' after the fact, considering that there was a contract and the work would, when finished, definitely see publication.

While completing details on the publication date for *The Sacred Fount* back in January 1901, Scribner's had sent £200 to Pinker on the *Wings* advance, but did not see the complete revised proofs until the end of April 1902 after Constable had used them for the English edition. As Pinker explained, "the book has been delayed by Mr. James's illness, and he wishes now to postpone it until the autumn,"[92] following up with four shipments during March and April of the proofs as they came to him from the printer. Constable patiently followed the

---

[89] Ibid. 66.

[90] Horne, *Henry James: A Life* 355.

[91] Vincec 73.

[92] Archives of Charles Scribner's Sons.

shuffling of corrected proofs from themselves to Pinker to Scribner's for the American edition. Constable then waited for Scribner's to set a publication date, as they wanted simultaneous publication, and wrote Pinker at the end of July 1902 asking for news, since they had originally expected to publish in October of the previous year: "We cannot find that there was any delay on our part whatever. You probably know that we were kept waiting a long time for copy, even after we had received some copy." The publisher had advertised the book in advance and was worried that further delay and uncertainty would affect sales: "We had hoped to give this book - the first with which Mr. Henry James has entrusted us - every possible chance, and it is a great disappointment to us that our plans are frustrated."[93]

Following his usual habit, James conveniently forgot that the publication delay was his fault and complained to Pinker, who knew very well what (or who) was the problem and could only attempt to appease both parties without implicating his client. *Wings* was finally published in both countries in August 1902, and James laid the blame for the delay squarely on Scribner's shoulders, complaining to his friend Lucy Clifford at the end of the month: "[*Wings*] was kept back these two months through the backwardness of *American* publisher,"[94] discounting his failure to deliver on time, first through his pursuit of *The Ambassadors* and then through illness earlier that year.

In Pinker's March 1902 letter to Scribner's he notes that he will be in New York at the beginning of April; it was during this visit that arrangements were made for Scribner's to publish James's new book of short stories, *The Better Sort* (contracts for this work as well as for *Wings* and the as yet unnamed *The Golden Bowl* are all dated April 11, 1902). In November 1902 Pinker notified the publisher that James had

---

[93] Henry James Collection.

[94] Vincec 81.

finished the manuscript and it had been sent to Methuen's printers, as Methuen was handling the English edition. No problems appear to have delayed the project for Scribner's, but as a collection of previously published short stories it would not have been as time consuming or open to difficulties as one of the author's long novels. *The Better Sort* was published on both sides of the Atlantic in February 1903 and Pinker recognized receipt of £162.2.9 from Scribner's on March 16, "being One Hundred Pounds on account on Mr. Henry James's new book of short stories, and £67.2.9 on account of royalties on 'The Wings of a Dove.'"[95]

Later that month, Scribner's was pleased to report that the short story volume was selling well, and in May pursued Pinker for validation of agreed upon details for James's next novels, following *The Ambassadors*: "your recent letters inform us that these will be published in England by Messrs. Methuen & Co. and that one is expected to appear in the Spring of 1904 and the other possibly in the Autumn of that year."[96] The first book, *The Golden Bowl*, would prove James's last novel, and the second, *The Sense of the Past*, would never be completed. Contact between Scribner's and Pinker appears suspended for nearly a year (during which *The Ambassadors* was published both as a book in England and America and as a twelve month long serial in the *North American Review*, not without trial to Pinker) before the agent contacted the publisher again about the novel that would become *The Golden Bowl*.

In February 1904 Pinker explained to Scribner's that while James had not yet finished his new novel, he would do so within five or six weeks and wished to publish that autumn. A month later, he acknowledged receipt of a £92.2.10 payment from the publisher, but for which title he did not specify. Three more months went by before Scribner's asked the

---

[95] Archives of Charles Scribner's Sons.

[96] Henry James Collection.

agent about *The Golden Bowl*; in July Pinker put them off, delivering the manuscript, finally, in August, at which point he admitted that while it might not be the usual time during the publishing process when payment would be extended, he needed to ask for it anyway as it would be "a convenience" to the author: "It is, of course, according to the terms of the contract, payable on the publication of the novel, but as Mr. James had anticipated an earlier appearance than is now possible, it would be more convenient to him not to wait until the exact date of publication."[97]

Three weeks later, James wrote Scribner's claiming that he would not write another long novel as "the best work of my life has, however, I think, gone into the G.B."[98] He seemed to have forgotten that the publisher was expecting another novel after *The Golden Bowl.* After Scribner's inquired as to whether the author wished his payments sent directly to him, he explained that "there are reasons, as it happens, why this check *should* go to Pinker."[99] The author's answer to the publisher's offer, while cryptic, validated his trust in and appreciation for the agent, who had been and would continue to handle payments and distribution of the same to the author's private bank accounts, for the rest of James's life and that of his own after the author's death.

Letters between Scribner's and Pinker regarding the publication date for *The Golden Bowl* apparently crossed in the mail a few days after James's instruction to Scribner's, with Scribner's dated September 20, 1904: "We are anxious to bring the novel out while Mr. James is here [between August 1904 and July 1905], so as to secure for it and for him the benefit of whatever additional sale may accrue from his presence in

---

[97] Archives of Charles Scribner's Sons.

[98] Horne, *Henry James: A Life* 403.

[99] Ibid. 404.

this country and the interest that naturally attaches thereto."[100] Pinker wrote the following day that the manuscript had been sent on August 5, and that he hoped that the publisher would suggest a publication date. Handwritten notes on this letter indicate that £200 was sent on October 4, in response to the request of the August 17 letter, and Pinker acknowledged the advance on October 14 while noting in a handwritten postscript that the English publisher, Methuen, would be unable to set up the novel in time for simultaneous publication in November, and that Methuen was counting on Scribner's to provide them with advance copies of the book.

Scribner's was able to publish in November, but Methuen, held up by the American publisher who was in turn held up by the author, did not publish until February 1905, although Scribner's did provide the necessary copies for copyright deposit on November 12. Pinker had written Scribner's in September asking for six advance copies of their edition for copyright purposes in America; the October letter reflects Methuen's (and in turn, Pinker's) anxiety over the necessity of obtaining these copies as soon as possible to deposit for copyright protection in England. James, meanwhile, had advance monies in his account from both publishers in October 1904, acquired by his agent's inexhaustible efforts, and was three months into his visit to America by the time the American edition appeared. Pinker continued his attention to the financial aspect of *The Golden Bowl* in June 1905, writing Scribner's that their royalty computation was faulty to James's disadvantage at twenty cents per copy, and asked for a check for the difference in the amount due his client. That twenty cents translates into approximately fifteen dollars in today's purchasing power, which could add up considerably.

Pinker proved himself interested in more than his client's financial concerns a few months later in a letter to Scribner regarding the

---

[100] Henry James Collection.

handling of an essay from what James believed was *Partial Portraits* (1888) but was being printed in an edition of Turgenieff by Dent, who claimed that they had purchased the material from Scribner's. He wrote on the same concern the very next day (October 5, 1905) specifically that the author was "distressed" that the piece was "torn from its setting"[101] without his consent. The agent asked for a halt to the English edition, and a letter on October 26 thanking the publisher for a quick response noted that the problem, as indicated by the previous two letters, was that the author felt the work "unsuited" to the use. No mention of money was made, as that was not what worried the author or agent; it was the author's name and reputation that called for protection in this situation.

James's trip to America from August 1904 to July 1905 began and ended with the idea of a collected edition of his work, a project suggested to Pinker by Edward Burlingame at Scribner's four years earlier. Pinker had met with the editor early in 1900 and a telegram from Burlingame in the New York Scribner's office on April 2, 1900 asks: "Would You Care on any terms to arrange for Collected Edition Henry James?" It stands to reason that a meeting with James's agent would prompt Burlingame to ask this after discussing the possibility with him. James had been thinking of a 'definitive' edition in which he could revise and explain his work, but he "deliberately confided his ambitions to no one (except, of course, his literary agent)."[102] He instructed Pinker to contact Scribner's about it, just as James was preparing to visit the country he had left 21 years earlier.

Pinker wrote Burlingame immediately, on August 3, 1904, stating that

---

[101] Archives of Charles Scribner's Sons.

[102] Anesko, Michael. "James in America: In Quest of (the) Material." *Cambridge Quarterly* 37 (2008): 5.

the communication was "personal" and specific to the "conversation about the collected edition of Mr. Henry James' books." He indicated that there had been "various proposals" from other publishers about such an edition, but that Scribner's would have first consideration, and by the way, James had a new novel "looming in the near future"[103] and was hoping for serial publication. While the prospect of the edition had originated with Burlingame, his enthusiasm for it had waned over the intervening years for a variety of reasons that included the "commercial situation" and the timeliness of the project, which had, four years earlier, a "psychological moment"[104] that had now passed.

On Pinker's end, there is no evidence to support his claim that "various proposals" had been made; only Scribner's had expressed interest. The agent pursued this remote opportunity, well aware that the editor's reluctance was a reflection of James's general lack of popularity and that a little white lie might be the key to pushing the editor into acceptance. While James toured America collecting material that would result in a series of essays and a book (*The American Scene*) for Harper & Brothers and Chapman & Hall, Pinker began the correspondence that Anesko calls the "treacherous complications"[105] of arranging the Edition de Luxe, or New York Edition, of James's work.[106] A decade

---

[103] Archives of Charles Scribner's Sons.

[104] Henry James Collection.

[105] Anesko, *Letters* 331.

[106] The construction of the New York Edition and the popularity of such editions at this time are dealt with in the collection of essays *Henry James's New York Edition: the Construction of Authorship*, Ed. David McWhirter; "Henry James and the Cultural Frame of the New York Edition" by Philip Horne in *The Culture of Collected Editions*, Ed. Andrew Nash; "The Architecture of Henry James's New York Edition" by Leon Edel, *New England Quarterly* 24 (1951); and "Henry James 'In the Wood': Sequence and Significance of His Literary Labors, 1905-1907" by Hershel Parker, *Nineteenth-Century Fiction* 38 (1984).

later, Pinker would write to Wells, insisting that "when I went to America and arranged the uniform edition of Henry James's books, the labour and time involved were altogether out of proportion to the commission involved, but for men of your caliber the work has to be done if you are presented to the public in an adequate worthy manner."[107] Again, the emphasis Pinker placed on the value of the material and the author's genius was primary over the financial return, or in this case, a lack thereof.

Pinker arrived in America in June 1905 with James's absolute permission to negotiate on his behalf: "If you have any definite view about anything, by which I mean about The Edition in particular, you may be able to break ground about it even before seeing me."[108] Pinker knew that his first step would have to be obtaining permissions from the various publishers of the works James wished to include in the edition. He began that same month with the American Macmillans who held rights in eleven titles, and received a positive response from company president George Brett on June 21, 1905, who asked only that the author pay the publisher one hundred pounds upfront, as "it represents the loss to us on our ledgers up to this time on our publication of these works by Mr. James."[109] Brett's agreement was a bittersweet one, amiable and yet with terms that reflected the popular failure of James's material, and Pinker, ever concerned for his client's financial end, wanted Scribner's to pay the fee rather than James. He explained to Charles Scribner that he had already told James that Scribner would make "this payment without charging it to Mr. James' royalty amount, and that if I can arrange in other cases for definite payments on a reasonable basis in

---

[107] Smith, David C. *The Correspondence of H.G. Wells, Volume 2: 1904-1918.* (London: Pickering, 1998) 415.

[108] Horne, *Henry James: A Life* 411.

[109] Archive of Charles Scribner's Sons.

lieu of royalty you will bear these charges also."[110] The day after Pinker penned this missive, Macmillan sent Scribner's a bill for £100. The contract for the edition, dated March 14, 1906, would carry different terms than those Pinker had outlined to Scribner's and to his client; chiefly and critically, that the payment to Macmillan's *would* come out of James's royalties from Scribner's.

James was not unaware of the difficulties Pinker would have collecting agreements from his previous publishers; after all, he had negotiated his own business affairs for decades and had employed Pinker to take such trouble off his hands. He assured the agent in June 1905: "Sorry I am for the up-hill moments, in New York, that you found yourself again condemned to. You will tell me more about them [doubtful], and I shall feel but the more obliged to you for having successfully dealt with them."[111] James left for England on July 5, 1905, relaxing on the ship's deck while revising his first novel, *Roderick Hudson,* for his new endeavor.

By mid-month he was back home, while Pinker remained stateside to pursue the amity (and written agreements) of the remaining publishers involved. James wrote a lengthy, specific prospectus for Scribner's regarding his hopes for "an honorable presentation" that would be as physically attractive as their Kipling edition along with the additional feature of individual introductions to each volume that would bear a "freely colloquial" and "confidential" manner that shared a history of the work and "frank critical talk about its subject, its origin, its place in the whole artistic chain, and embodying, in short, whatever of interest there may be to be said about it."[112] He left the financial details to

---

[110] Ibid. handwritten

[111] Philip Horne, *Henry James and Revision: The New York Edition* (Oxford: Clarendon, 1990) 6.

[112] Archives of Charles Scribner's Sons.

Pinker, who was finding Harper, which held fourteen titles, more than considerate: "At the request of Mr. Henry James, we take pleasure in extending to you the privilege of including in your proposed collective edition of his works, the books written by him which we have published and copyrighted."[113]

The ease with which Harper accepted Pinker's proposal was soon to be overshadowed by the militant objections of Houghton Mifflin less than two months later in October 1905. The problem was similar to that with Heinemann five years earlier: "the method inaugurated by literary brokers of pitting one house against another and selling their client to the highest bidder is not one to be encouraged."[114] The Houghton titles, however, had been negotiated by the author himself, and his own habit of 'pitting' publishers to his own profit is what had brought about these troubles, not the efforts of his agent. Scribner's contacted Pinker with the unsettling development and Pinker attempted to place the responsibility for resolving the issue back on Scribner's: "I should be very sorry indeed to have to go to Mr. James and tell him that the negotiations had fallen through with yourselves, as he had settled down quite happily to the idea that his affairs were in your good hands."[115]

Pinker used James as a threat; it was implicit that the business arrangements must be continued without disturbing the content author at his work. Disturbing James would be a last resort for the agent and as Horne notes, "James himself, hard at work in Rye, was not directly bothered with these troubles, which Pinker muffled for him."[116] Fortunately, 'these troubles' were resolved by the end of November by a royalty split between Houghton Mifflin and James after George Mifflin

---

[113] Ibid.

[114] Horne, *Henry James and Revision* 7.

[115] Archives of Charles Scribner's Sons.

[116] Horne, *Henry James and Revision* 7.

insisted on his desire to be agreeable as to terms, although "we are not under ordinary circumstances favorable to a policy which scatters the writings of an author among various houses, only ultimately to bring them altogether into a uniform edition. Such a policy does not seem to us to be fair to the original publishers of the books."[117]

Fairness, of course, was not Pinker's concern. On December 5, 1905, Scribner's sent Pinker a draft of the agreement for the edition. James wrote his agent on the same day "glad in fact not to have to think of the matter, as my actual work makes all due demand on my wits," thanking Pinker for the "patience, ingenuity and diplomacy you have, in the whole matter, I am sure, been putting at my service."[118] He might have felt 'sure' but in reality, he had no idea what sort of insult to his profession and compromises to James's financial reward Pinker was having to accept to get James's much desired project off the ground, or the manipulative threats the agent was using to fulfill his client's wishes.

Pinker and James's relief was short-lived, however, when trouble with Herbert Stone, the American publisher of two of the titles to be included in the edition, *In the Cage* and *What Maisie Knew*, crept up only a few weeks later. Scribner's discovered the problem during an exchange with Stone on another project when Stone revealed; "I am quite at a loss as to understand Mr. Pinker's statement in regard to our rights in the books by Henry James. We purchased 'In a Cage' outright, and there was no question of a limited period in the contract for 'What Maisie Knew.'"[119]

Within a week after receiving Stone's letter, Scribner's alerted Pinker to Stone's claim, which would present a problem if the author wanted

---

[117] Archives of Charles Scribner's Sons.

[118] Horne, *Henry James and Revision* 9.

[119] Archives of Charles Scribner's Sons.

to include either book as planned. This difficulty did not dampen Scribner's interest in the edition: letters regarding the contract crossed in the mail, the first from Pinker to the publisher verifying that Harper would not charge for permissions while Macmillan would, payment to be covered by Scribner's (which would not be in the final agreement), and a rather anxious missive two days afterwards from Scribner's to Pinker, with worries about the agent's failure to communicate regarding the contract and asking for a cable upon receipt, which Pinker sent on February 10. 1906.

Scribner's contacted Fox, Duffield & Company in New York, who set Stone's claims to rest for both Scribner's and Pinker in March 1906: "We have purchased the Stone publications and have discovered no reason why these books should not have been transferred to us. We shall be obliged to you for any statement that you may be good enough to make to us."[120] Six days later, Scribner's agreed to cover the Macmillan fees upfront (again, charging against James's royalties after publication) and sent a revised contract to Pinker, verifying the Duffield ownership of the two Stone titles and noting that "we have made the desired increase of royalty on the Macmillan books as suggested and send contracts, one of which please return with Mr. James's signature. We shall now prepare to proceed with the work on the edition on receipt of 'copy' for volume one."[121] While the agent may have had to agree to the coverage of the Macmillan fees by the author's royalties, he had at least been able to obtain an increase in those royalties to hopefully cover the fee more quickly and thus provide for a profit for James sooner rather than later.

Pinker returned the signed contract on March 26 and allowed that he and Duffield were in communication; on the 28th he wrote again stating that James did indeed want the two books held by Duffield

---

[120] James B. Pinker and Son: Collection of Papers, 1893-1940.

[121] Ibid.

included in the edition. Duffield wrote Pinker in July assuring him that "we do not wish to oppose him [Scribner], or Mr. James, in the matter" and would "be glad to sign any suitable agreement you may send us."[122] In September 1906 Duffield again wrote suggesting Pinker draft a contract providing for payment to the publisher for plates, as "the sales of the two novels are not large, [and] we should be considerably out of pocket"[123] if they were not reimbursed in some way to compensate for the cost of initial production. Duffield was willing to cooperate but still understandably concerned about the house's loss concerning their investment in James's work, much like Macmillan.

In the midst of acquiring James's signature on the revised Scribner's contract and writing Fox, Duffield and Scribner's regarding the Stone situation, Pinker began contacting English publishers regarding the edition. He tried to interest Constable, and while the publisher considered the possibility, he wanted more information with which to make a decision on such an endeavor. Pinker informed Scribner's in March 1906 that he had approached Constable and that Scribner's would be hearing from the English house, with the expectation that Scribner's would be able to answer practical production questions. Over a year later, Constable contacted the agent, asking again for clarification that was not forthcoming from the American publisher, including information on the securing of copyrights and the pricing of sheets and royalties.

Scribner's would continue to leave Constable in the lurch, refusing to make a commitment to details until they had actually produced the books and could state a definite figure based on expenses; they also expected a large order (at least 100 sets) from the English publisher, who

---

[122] Letters Sent to James B. Pinker Concerning Henry James.

[123] Henry James Collection.

explained early on that he would only order sets of ten to 25 as needed. When 1907 came to an end without any settlement as to the English edition, Pinker must have pushed Constable on an emotional level that he felt would bring about the results needed to ensure publication. In January 1908, Constable explained his stance while remaining unmoved by the agent's attempt to manipulate him into agreement: "I am very sorry and a little surprised that you appear to think that we should have treated you or Mr. Henry James in any way that he or you could resent." He noted that for two years he had waited for information on the edition that he needed in order to make a commitment to publish, including production style, number of volumes, and price, along with the assurance that the copyright owners had all consented to the use of the works involved.

Constable also wondered about any of James's work that would be issued after the edition was complete; would those be included afterwards? After looking at the terms and conditions finally offered by Scribner's, Constable had "considered this proposition very carefully" and realized that it was not practical to pay what the American publisher wanted for sheets. He was worried about simultaneous publication and the possibility of cheaper volumes issued separately in America at a later date, which would undermine sales of the edition, which he wanted to be specifically limited, and so "of special value." "We feel sure that when you have read this letter and considered it you will exonerate us of any intention of treating the matter as if it were 'of small account,' either to Mr. Henry James, or yourself, or we may add, to ourselves."[124]

In February 1908, English publisher John Murray (who had not previously published James's work) notified Scribner's London agent Lemuel Bangs that Pinker had been negotiating with him about the edition, but like Constable, he would not want more than 25 sets to

------

[124] Ibid.

start, as "I hope that we may sell more than this, but as we are not very confident, we do not want to risk more than this."[125] Pinker wrote Scribner's with that detail on the same day Murray wrote Bangs, and received an irritated response from the publisher, who said that they were "disappointed at the smallness" of the proposed order and wished to decline the offer, and furthermore, if Pinker continued to have difficulty finding an English publisher, "we should prefer to market our own edition in England."[126] Since neither Constable nor Murray wanted more than 25 sets, as Anesko notes, Scribner's "now regretted leaving the disposal of English rights to the Edition to the hands of James's agent. But whose interest was Pinker commissioned to protect after all: author or publisher? If, to James, Pinker had become 'a blessing unspeakable,' to Scribner he was just an unspeakable nuisance."[127] Scribner's was, however, the cause of Pinker's failure, as they had created difficulties with Constable. The American publisher gave the job to Bangs, who of course acted unquestionably on their behalf, resulting in a contract with the English Macmillans, who did make the desired 100 sets of sheets order but only bound and sold a fraction of them, while the rest was used as wrapping paper during World War II. At this point, however, no one working with James or his agent should have been surprised that Pinker was his author's man and no one else's.

Concurrent to the signing of the contract with Scribner's in March 1906, Pinker sent James's revised *Roderick Hudson*, on which the author worked during and since his return trip from America eight months

---

[125] Archives of Charles Scribner's Sons.

[126] James B. Pinker and Son: Collection of Papers, 1893-1940.

[127] Michael Anesko, "Ambiguous Allegiances: Conflicts of Culture and Ideology in the Making of the New York Edition" *Henry James's New York Edition: the Construction of Authorship* Ed. David McWhirter (Stanford: Stanford UP, 1995): 83.

earlier, to the publisher. The work was sent in two packages, the first of which was never received by Scribner's and the second damaged in transport, the wrapping in shreds, but the part the publisher did receive was troubling due to the author's "interlineations and emendations" which were "so numerous" and "intricate" that the printer's cost would be "very considerable and serious" and the publisher feared as well the "effect on the cordial co-operation of the printers if we began with such difficult 'copy.'"[128] Scribner asked for a typewritten copy, although the publisher could have the manuscript in hand typewritten with the expense charged to James. The author wrote to Scribner himself in May to offer to have the revised manuscript typewritten, but not without insisting on a promise that the printers, who would benefit from the clarity of the typewritten pages, would set the work as written: "I beg the Compositors to *adhere irremoveably* to my punctuation & *never* to insert death-dealing commas."[129]

As if he did not have enough work regarding the edition already, Pinker then became involved with the frontispiece photography for the edition although the art editor at *Scribner's Magazine*, Joseph Hawley Chapin, claimed to know the photographer, Alvin Langdon Coburn, and said he would handle the touchy problems regarding fees, which Chapin found excessive. He hoped to negotiate a lump sum to cover the photographer's work on the edition as a whole, and told Pinker that he would be glad "to correspond directly with Mr. Coburn."[130] In February 1907, however, Chapin instructed Pinker to tell Coburn that any work he completed for the James edition would be the property of Scribner's and as such, not available for Coburn to sell elsewhere. The editor explained that he would contact Coburn himself but "in the

---

[128] Henry James Collection.

[129] Horne, *Henry James: A Life* 432.

[130] Henry James Collection.

meantime you can, of course, let Mr. Coburn know how we feel about it."[131]

Before the first volume of the edition even appeared, James expressed his frustration with the project to his brother William in October 1907: "it will be an immense relief to me when the famous Edition is off my hands . . . the prefaces are very difficult to make *right*, absolutely and utterly, as they supremely have to be."[132] Pinker did his best to shield his client from further stress, and in December 1907 they were both rewarded with the physical proof of the fruits of their labors. Scribner's printed 1500 copies of volumes one through ten, and would go on to print 1000 each of volumes eleven through 24.

The publisher sent Pinker "with our compliments, one copy of the first and second volumes, which are now ready, of the new edition of the Novels and Tales of Henry James. We are forwarding direct to Mr. James a copy of each of these two volumes."[133] James told Scribner that he was "serenely content"[134] with the finished product and wrote on the last day of the year to his agent: "I rejoice that you are in as punctual possession as I am of the two beautiful volumes (for beautiful I hold them to be), in which I quite agree with you that we may take pleasure & pride."[135] The 'we' is very telling; James clearly felt that Pinker was a vital part of making the edition happen, and saw the result as a joint effort of his own artistic craft and the agent's business acumen. The shared ownership James saw of the two volumes was a reflection of his appreciation and his acknowledgement of Pinker's work.

---

[131] Letters Sent to James B. Pinker Concerning Henry James.

[132] Edel, *Henry James: Letters* 467.

[133] Henry James Collection.

[134] Edel, *Henry James: Letters* 484.

[135] Horne, *Henry James: A Life* 454.

Pinker spent the next year working on (unsuccessful) negotiations for the English edition and attempting to obtain a financial return for James (while muddling through a stressful time in his relationship with Joseph Conrad, previously noted), who had been working diligently on the edition without payment. The agent wrote Charles Scribner in September 1908, explaining that he had received "practically nothing" for James over the past year, and asked for any funds that were coming due for the author. He also asked for the publisher's discretion, since "Mr. James does not know I am writing to you as he is sensitive on these matters and I would rather he thought it was your own prompting."[136]

Pinker did not need credit for any results he might obtain, as his only concern was to obtain money for his client while James remained blissfully unaware that his agent was begging on his behalf. Scribner took a few weeks to send a letter of regret and explanation that focused primarily on the unfortunate fact that the sales of the edition had not yet covered the cost of the Macmillan fee, although "the edition is very highly praised by all and there must be a great many admirers of Mr. James's work who will eventually purchase it."[137] The permission fee was not fully covered until February 1909; meanwhile, the 'high praise' noted by Scribner did not make James feel financially secure, and James was stunned in October 1908 by the low royalty payment from the edition. He guessed that the figures worked out to be $211 but was confused by the royalty statement, as he relied on Pinker generally to understand such business.

James' income for 1908 was the lowest it had been in 25 years, in contrast to the first eight years of Pinker's service, which had resulted in an average of twice (if not more) as much per year than it had been before James hired the agent, who had been able to sell him rather

---

[136] Archives of Charles Scribner's Sons.

[137] Ibid.

effectively in spite of a lower demand for his work. James admonished himself in a letter to Pinker when the reality of the low royalties set in: "I have been living in a fool's paradise."[138] The last preface of the Collected Edition (for *The Golden Bowl*) was complete and off James's hands in March 1909 after much emotional and physical stress over the revisions and prefaces, upon both of which he elaborated to friends and family excessively. The sizes of the volumes were prohibitive to profit, with prefaces longer than the publishers expected and difficulties that were financially taxing to all involved.

All was quiet between the James and Scribner camps for over a year except for statements and checks on James's account until Pinker approached Scribner's in April 1910 about a book of five stories the author was considering for autumn publication. This collection, *The Finer Grain*, was an easy production, with publication in October of that year after a ready agreement and payment of James's requested £100 advance. A year later, however, Pinker's efforts to negotiate terms for *The Outcry* met with some resistance. The agent asked for a serial run in *Scribner's Magazine* as well as an advance of £300. The advance figure was based on the contract for *The Golden Bowl*, which stated that the publisher would pay up to that amount for James's next title if *The Golden Bowl* earned enough to cover it, but as Charles Scribner noted in his reply to the current request, the first novel had been issued in two volumes at a higher price and as such, increased the royalty amount. *The Outcry* was a much smaller novel and would bring a lower price with corresponding royalties. He did agree to an advance of £200 with any royalties over that amount to be issued after the first three months to satisfy James's need for immediate financial gain. Scribner wrote in August 1911 in response to a request from Pinker to delay book publication while the agent explored the possibility of serial sale, but

---

[138] Horne, *Henry James: A Life* 468.

this did not come to pass and Scribner's, eager to publish the volume, issued it in October, along with the £200 advance.

When James began working on the three manuscripts that would become his autobiographical trilogy, his initial plan was to use his late brother William's letters to focus on a biographical concern for his famous philosopher-psychologist sibling, but he deferred on that use for the first title, *A Small Boy and Others*, which he finished in early September 1912. William's son Henry wrote to his uncle that month about the failure of his father's correspondence to appear in the work, placing blame on Pinker, but James did not agree. He explained to his nephew that the younger Henry should "banish from your mind every view of my relation with him [Pinker] in which his having anything to say to the nature of my work itself" as the agent "would never in the world presume to cross any such line, or should I dream of allowing him to - our relations are altogether on the other side of it: on the basis of my own stuff done in my own way, where his cognizance of it only begins."[139]

Pinker had informally negotiated a £500 advance each for *Small Boy* and its sequel, *Notes of a Son and Brother*, and was dismayed by a letter from Scribner in December 1912 refuting that amount, claiming that he had named £100 when the matter was discussed. The publisher did sympathize with the agent on the difficulty of dealing with James: "It is an awkward situation if you named the larger sum to Mr. James but I do not think we should be expected to make such a radical change in our agreement."[140] Pinker must have sent a reply that expressed his deep dislike of the low advance proposed, as Scribner sent a cable on January 8, 1913 stating "Greatly regret James misunderstanding

---

[139] Edel, *Henry James: Letters* 794.

[140] Henry James Collection.

cannot accept your contracts but will advance five hundred on two books together." The agent wrote back the following day with the news that he had pulled out the big guns and spoke to the author about the trouble, which was always a last resort: "I was anxious to avoid this for various reasons, the most important being that he is now very much better in health, and immersed in work."

The advance, as always, was incredibly important to James, and the agent explained to Scribner that he had told the author that "I feel sure you would agree to pay the Five Hundred Pounds on publication of the first book this spring, so that as he had counted on that sum his plans will not be disorganized immediately."[141] The publisher wrote back on January 13 accepting Pinker's terms as Pinker had assured James that he would, in short, agree to pay James £500 on the publication of *A Small Boy* and *Notes of a Son and Brother*. On April 1, 1913, Scribner's sent Pinker a draft for the £500 along with a copy of *A Small Boy and Others*; the amount was just what Pinker asked for at the time James expected it, regardless of the shuffling of contractual language. James had the money when he expected it, thanks to the agent, who managed to coerce an extra £300 out of the publisher, who originally planned to pay £100 for each advance.

At the same time James finished *A Small Boy*, Charles Scribner sent a proposal for "another great novel" to both the author and agent, noting that the terms might be "somewhat unusual,"[142] namely the payment of $8000 for all rights to it. What the publisher did not disclose was the source of such a large sum, James's friend Edith Wharton, who was worried about the older author's financial situation after he had "lost almost no occasion over many years to complain to her about his

---

[141] Archives of Charles Scribner's Sons.

[142] Edel, *Henry James: Letters* 789.

poverty, to highlight the gap between the comparatively impoverished hospitality he could offer at Lamb House"[143] and her residences. Her concerns led her to instruct Scribner's to redirect the $8000 from her own substantial royalty account with them and offer it to James.

Pinker answered for his client, agreeing to the terms, but the publisher and Wharton were not happy to have Pinker profit by the arrangement, as Wharton's aim was to enlarge James's coffers, not the agent's. The publisher explained his stance, without reference to the nature of the original offer, to Pinker, noting that "there has been no work on your part,"[144] and Pinker left the decision to James, keeping his suspicions about the contribution from Wharton to himself to save James the embarrassment of knowing that others believed he was destitute and also leaving the author free to accept the sum for work expected, rather than as charity, which would of course make him feel more financially secure.

James's ongoing obsession with his financial state and comments to concerned friends like Wharton led Pinker to write to the author's nephew Henry in January 1912 to inquire as to the true state of affairs and was assured that "this is no occasion for him [James] to vex his mind about finances at all."[145] While the author's concern seemed inexplicable to his nephew, it was very real to James himself and caused him distress, so much that even though he expressed some hesitation about the Scribner arrangement to Pinker, primarily over the surrender of copyright as he had a "very deep instinct of objection to it,"[146] he did agree and accepted $4000 from Scribner's on February 28, 1913, sent to his agent, of course, who kept his usual 10% fee at the author's

---

[143] Kaplan 547.

[144] Edel, *Henry James: Letters* 792.

[145] Letters Concerning the James Family.

[146] Edel, *Henry James: Letters* 626.

insistence.

In early 1914 James collected previously published essays for a volume called *Notes on Novelists*, which was contracted to Scribner's in January and published in October. Scribner's attempted to obtain the Canadian rights for *Notes* because "we usually have the Canadian market on these books"[147] but Pinker had to remove that stipulation in the contract, just as he had before for *The Golden Bowl*: "I am very sorry that I cannot give you the Canadian market. I tried to get it in your agreement, but a very satisfactory agreement on this side [Dent] was dependent on it, and I wanted particularly to get Mr. James all that I can on this book."[148]

A year later, in January 1915, months after *Notes* appeared, James complained to Pinker about his advance, or lack thereof: "I infer from the limits of Scribner's cheque [his semiannual royalty statement] that I get nothing at all from him 'down' . . . on those *Notes!*"[149] The next day Pinker wrote the publisher reminding them that he had not received the appropriate advance, and two weeks later, £256 was sent. This would be the last advance James would receive from Scribner's.

Less than six months after James's death in 1916, Scribner's approached Pinker about publishing the author's last autobiographical piece, *The Middle Years*, asserting that there was no reason to delay, as they wanted to issue portions in their magazine as well as the entirety of it as a volume. Two articles at the rate of $250 each, editor Edward Burlingame offered, as he was "sincerely interested, as you are, in keeping Mr. James's work together and in seeing what he had left

---

[147] Archives of Charles Scribner's Sons.

[148] Ibid.

[149] Edel, *Henry James: Letters* 733.

used to the best advantage."[150] The agent, of course, negotiated a higher payment for the articles, and in February 1917 the publisher took on the publication of the two unfinished novels left by the author, *The Sense of the Past* and *The Ivory Tower*, explaining that they did not feel an advance was appropriate. Pinker agreed, as he no longer had need of the 'down' for his worried client. He accepted their usual 20% royalty rate and insisted that Scribner's pay a share of the editing fee, of which the publisher had to be reminded in February 1918: "I shall be very much obliged if you will let me have a cheque for the fee due to Mr. Percy Lubbock in payment of his work of editing the Henry James books."[151] The payment was issued on March 19.

Later that year Pinker found himself in the midst of price negotiations between Scribner's and Collins, the English publisher of *The Sense of the Past* and *The Ivory Tower*, who would be setting up the type and selling the sheets to Scribner's for their use in America. He also attempted to mollify Scribner's when the English Macmillans sought to issue a cheaper collected edition of James's works, which distressed Scribner because of the possible dent it would make in the sales of the New York Edition, which had all but come to a halt. Scribner complained to James's nephew Henry in November 1919 about the use of the prefaces, which were "of course written for the New York Edition and we think they should only be used in connection therewith."[152] Looking out for James had always been Pinker's priority and as such, allowed the agent to override Scribner's objections and pursue the path that would gain the most exposure for the author's work and profit to his estate. As Anesko notes, "Macmillan was ultimately persuaded by Pinker and Percy Lubbock that a cheaper - and more inclusive - edition of James's

---

[150] Henry James Collection.

[151] Archives of Charles Scribner's Sons.

[152] Letters Sent to James B. Pinker Concerning Henry James.

works would find buyers."[153] *The Novels and Tales of Henry James*, a more accessible version of the Scribner edition by virtue of its lower price, was published from 1921 to 1923, a continuing result of Pinker's efforts even after the agent himself died in early 1922.

While the New York Edition was a disappointment to all involved, it was not because of a lack of effort or expertise on the part of the agent. While James continued to make difficulties for the publishers' schedules and clearly had no regard for contractual details, his agent successfully 'begged indulgence' for him, allowing the author to continue writing, for the most part undisturbed, in the manner that kept him productive. He also handled the trouble caused by James's previous 'flittings' between publishers, which occurred long before Pinker became involved and caused the most problems with the Collected Edition. How and why the arrangement for Scribner's to pay the Macmillan fee without damage to James's royalties fell through is a mystery. Clearly, Pinker had taken James's financial concerns into account, as always, and the correspondence between the agent and publisher is clear on the matter.

While Pinker may have withheld information from James when such would have been disruptive to his client, he was not in the habit of lying to the author, particularly regarding the terms of his contracts. Sometime between June 1905 and March 1906 when the contract was actually signed, with the stipulation that the royalties would first be used to cover the Macmillan fee, the terms changed; with the evidence of Pinker's business habits at hand, one might guess that he agreed to do this on James's behalf because it became an issue that may have possibly stopped the edition altogether. Keeping James in print and in this case, with a fresh perspective by the author himself, would have been a better deal than losing the opportunity over £100.

---

[153] Anesko, *Ambiguous* 88.

No one expected the edition to fail so miserably, so Pinker's estimation, as it most likely was, that the royalties would amount to enough to minimize the loss of the fee was not inordinate. To his credit, he did negotiate an increase in royalties to assist in that regard. Earlier in the Scribner relationship, he had successfully continued to do as James bid insofar as obtaining advances before publication, in this case, for *The Golden Bowl*, so that the author had money at hand for his trip to America; his primary concern, as always regarding advances, for the author's 'convenience.' His difficulties with Scribner's advances came after the New York Edition, when the publisher could see that their investment in James's work had become riskier than they might prefer. Pinker used his business knowledge to obtain an unusually rewarding contract for the material James went to America to gather and produce. *The American Scene* would be a complicated endeavor that took all of Pinker's negotiating skills as well as his patience and that of the publishers involved. James's excitement over his travel writings would be dampened by publishers' mistakes, which upset him as he worked on the volumes of the New York Edition, work that was ultimately, in James's lifetime, without reward.

Harper & Brothers and Chapman & Hall

Pinker's continued success in obtaining advances that would, as if he could almost predict, not be met by actual sales, as well as the author's ongoing inability to produce on demand was demonstrated by the fantastic payments acquired for James's collection of travel essays, *The American Scene.* James's emotional responses to the careless handling of his material by publishers show exactly why Pinker preferred to keep the author sheltered from publication troubles. Even when James's anger was understandable in a particular situation, his tendency to overreact in an extreme fashion was obviously worth avoiding if at all possible, as it distracted the author from his writing, but it was also useful to Pinker as a threat to those who would want to avoid dealing with the author when he was in such a state. Ultimately, this behavior created more work for Pinker, namely that of placating and encouraging James in order to keep him producing regardless of whatever stress the business side of the work was giving the agent.

James's long-standing relationship with Harper & Brothers dated back to the publication of the enormously popular *Daisy Miller* in 1879 and, as noted earlier, caused some difficulty for Pinker with Methuen during the publication process for *The Ambassadors* in 1903. In the spring of 1904, Pinker approached them regarding a collection of travel impressions James intended to write about his visit to America, to be undertaken in August of that year. As Anesko notes, Pinker negotiated a "lucrative" contract not only for this book but also for a novel to follow, along with the serialization of both volumes. The travel title would bring James £80 per article (with the promise to publish at least eight) to be published in Harper's *North American Review*, and the book would net a £400 advance on royalties of 15% on the first 5000 copies, raised to 20% thereafter, on a list price of $3. The novel (presumably *The Ivory Tower*) would be serialized for £1500 if placed in *Harper's Magazine*, which enjoyed a British circulation as well as American, or £500 if published in the *North American Review*, which only sold in America, and a £200 advance on the book.

In order to help his friend earn the money to finance his trip, Howells managed arrangements for James to speak in a series of lectures on such topics as 'the novel' and Balzac at women's clubs during the stops on his American tour. The author would need time to amass his material for the contracted articles and volume, during which "from both his agent and his publisher, James demanded patience."[154] This demand was, of course, not unique to this particular project.

Pinker was able to come to terms with Chapman & Hall, the publisher of Dickens and Thackeray, in May 1905 for the English market after some difficulty, as he was determined to find a publisher who would offer serial as well as book publication along the lines of the Harper arrangement. The £200 for the use of material in their *Fortnightly Review* and £250 in advance of 15% royalties on the books (with a list price of 12/6) were considerably less than Harper's generous terms, but with the American figures so high Pinker could afford to accept what was offered in order to ensure that James's material would be in print on both sides of the Atlantic. Little did the agent or his author know that the edition that brought James more money would bring him much disappointment and frustration.

---

[154] Anesko, "James in America" 7.

James and Pinker were both engaged in work on and regarding the New York Edition with Scribner from the time of these agreements into the next year; it is no surprise that the beginning of 1906 brought inquiries from Chapman & Hall editor Nelson Ward to Pinker: "Can you give me any idea how we stand with regard to Mr. Henry James's book?"[155] and again in June: "We have not yet received the MS. of Mr. Henry James's book. I should very much like to set this in hand as soon as convenient to himself, as the printers are apt to get so full a little bit later on. Have you yet heard anything from him on the subject?"[156]

In late summer, Ward sent a handwritten postcard to Pinker: "Still without 'copy' for Mr. Henry James's book and I am leaving for my holiday next week and anxious to put it in hand before I go. Can you drop him a line? We really ought to get to work now."[157] Ward's rising panic reached a head when he did not find the book waiting for him when he returned from his vacation, and he lost his usual respectful treatment of the author, if only by calling him 'sensitive' in another handwritten missive to the agent: "I have just returned from my holiday to find that not a line of Mr. Henry James's MS. has been received. Do, pray, get him to send it along. I know he is sensitive and all that; but a contract is a contract, and we must have the book this autumn."[158]

One day later, Ward begged again: "As you are going to spend the week-end with Henry James, do you think you could get him to let us have a brief account or description of his book for our Autumn list? He could say briefly what the book aims at being, and I could put in

---

[155] James B. Pinker and Son: Collection of Papers, 1893-1940.

[156] Letters Sent to James B. Pinker Concerning Henry James.

[157] Ibid.

[158] Ibid.

the complimentary adjectives. I hope you can get him to do this."[159] While Chapman & Hall had not published a book by James before now, the firm was obviously aware that the best way to approach the author regarding difficulties was through his agent (Ward knew James was "sensitive and all that"), who had a reputation himself of being the party best able to influence the author's performance and had dealt with the publisher before regarding the work of other writers.

James wanted publication as soon as possible after he sent his last chapter to Pinker in the fall of 1906: "I feel, perhaps a bit nervously, as if I didn't know what they might be capable of if hustled. Let us hustle enough therefore, but not too much!"[160] James was, in all honesty, really not in a position to expect 'hustling' from other parties, but he believed that bypassing Harper proofs, which he thought would be acceptable as they were created from the Chapman corrections, would save time, which it did.

The proofs for *The American Scene* traveled from Chapman & Hall to James then back to Chapman & Hall with the author's important emendation of running heads that changed every two pages. Pinker had written Harper in August 1906, a month before James sent in his last chapter, pushing for book publication and allowing that "if Florida [the last chapter] is to be included in the book that would postpone its publication until next year. This Mr. James is most anxious to avoid . . . I am sending to the London publishers the complete copy for the book,

---

[159] Additional Letters Concerning the James Family. Pinker often socialized with his clients, including James, Conrad, and the writing team of Somerville and Ross, Violet Martin and Edith Somerville, the former a friend from their work together at *Black & White* who called Pinker a "great rider to hounds" with a fondness for stamp collecting: "he and I used to race to get the foreign stamps out of the editor's wastepaper basket for our collections." Hunt, Violet. *I Have This to Say: The Story of My Flurried Years.* (New York: Boni and Liveright, 1926) 10.

[160] Henry James Collection.

and will get corrected proofs for you, so that there may be no necessity to send proofs of your book to Mr. James for correction."[161]

While getting James to provide the manuscript in a timely fashion for production purposes was stressful for Ward, he was quick to display a genuine respect for the author's work: "By no means let Henry James cut his last chapter. We don't want to throw gold fringe into the gutter. Let us have every word he has written."[162] This desire to be faithful to James's words was the opposite feeling and intention towards the author's material than the one held by Harper. The American publisher was beginning to add to Ward's stress by asking for a delay in publication date in order to have a simultaneous release in both countries, a request Ward did not expect or understand: "Surely as the whole of this material of Henry James's book has appeared in America [as a serial] and is therefore copyright we are not going to be asked to hold the book back simply to meet Harper's date."[163]

Ward's desire to publish the volume in the fall of 1906 fell to the demands and mismanagement of the work by Harper along with Pinker's attempts to please the author. On January 2, 1907 Ward wrote Pinker that he had only just discussed the situation with Chapman & Hall managing director Evelyn Waugh and "we have decided to publish Mr. Henry James's book on the 30th January, and have communicated this decision to Messrs. Harper & Brothers."[164] Chapman & Hall's 1500 copy edition of *The American Scene* was issued in "burgundy red buckram, lettered in gilt on front cover and spine"[165] and carried the full weight of James's words at 472 pages. The American edition suffered

---

[161] Archives of Harper & Brothers, 1817-1914.

[162] Additional Letters Concerning the James Family.

[163] Ibid.

[164] Letters Sent to James B. Pinker Concerning Henry James.

[165] Edel, *Bibliography* 133.

under the pressure of James's interest in quick publication and Pinker's support of the same, but more so because of Harper's lack of care with James's material, specifically his corrections.

On February 7, 1907, 2500 copies were issued in "cobalt blue vertical-ribbed cloth, lettered in gilt on front cover and spine"[166] and allowed the American publishers to save time in their own manner, namely, by ignoring the corrections and running heads, and by adding a line to each page in order to shorten the volume, which was longer than they had anticipated. At 446 pages, it was missing the last section (five pages) of the Florida (final) chapter along with the corrections made to the English proofs. Pinker had stated that James didn't need to see the Harper proofs, but that was with the understanding that the publisher would take note of the author's changes to the *English* proofs. James was incensed in a letter to Pinker in April: "I extremely resent their whole indifference, cavalier, uncivil treatment of my stuff, as if it were beneath their notice."[167] He was shocked, as after such a long relationship with Harper he had no reason to expect the publisher to be 'indifferent' to his material; however, the changes in the firm over nearly three decades, including a bankruptcy and change in presidential and editorial hands, should have given sufficient reason to reconsider. The author wrote another complaint to his agent nine days later, on May 5, referring to Harper's failure to pay attention to his corrections as "fairly monstrous" and explaining why he hadn't contacted the publisher directly when the offending book arrived at his doorstep: "While my interests were under discussion with them I thought it not right to put in my oar. But it's a point on which I do hate they should go 'Scott free!'"[168] With a

---

[166] Edel, *Bibliography* 134.

[167] Archives of Harper & Brothers, 1817-1914.

[168] Edel, *Henry James: Letters* 448.

Scot on the case, they certainly would not.[169]

Pinker, 'rowing' on James's behalf, added pressure by enclosing the author's scathing April letter in a missive of his own to the London office of Harper's, which, per usual, contacted the New York office with the communication. The agent asked that the "guilty person" be called to account for "his mutilation of the volume by the wanton suppression of the page head-lines," quoting James and reiterating that the running heads were "essential."[170] When this letter went without response, Pinker approached the problem from a different perspective, writing again to say that James wished to cancel the arrangement he had with Harper for the serial and volume rights of his novel. The author believed that "he is anticipating your wishes, as he is certainly consulting his own,"[171] including his annoyance over the current difficulty.

This finally attracted the notice of Harper & Brothers president George Harvey, who wrote to the author two weeks later, begging him to "drop over these offenses the mantle of charity, of which I observe you modestly claim a fair share"[172] while assuring him that no one at the house intended any discourtesy. Harvey did not mention the time and effort James's changes had caused his firm in the production of the work, during which they were rushed by the agent at James's request. This apology must have been acceptable to James, as less than two months later Harper was responding to a request by James to defer the short novel *Julia Bride*, discussed in letters the previous autumn and promised to Harper's as both a serial and a book, until the publication

---

[169] While Pinker is often referred to as Scottish ("a small lively Scotsman" according to Compton Mackenzie) there is some discrepancy as to his heritage. He was born in London and his mother may have been Welsh, according to J.H. Stape in "Pinker of Agents: A Family History of James Brand Pinker" *The Conradian* (34) 1: 111-143.

[170] Archives of Harper & Brothers, 1817-1914.

[171] Ibid.

[172] Ibid.

of the long novel.

From the last few months of 1907 through the spring of 1908, however, Pinker was under pressure to pursue an English publisher for the Collected Edition and James was struggling with the prefaces for the same. Correspondence with Harper's regarding *Julia Bride* came to a halt for over six months, until Harper's issued the story as a serial in March and April 1908 in *Harper's Magazine*. Pinker approached the publisher with James's request for another deferment, which posed some difficulties as they had already produced it as a serial and had it set in type for book publication. Further delay at that point would not be in their interest, but they were willing to comply with the request to please the emotionally fragile author and the agent who did nothing to mitigate James's dramatics.

The Collected Edition took James's attention for the next year, during which he saw the financial failure of his efforts while still working to complete it, and Pinker finally returned to the *Julia Bride* discussion with Harper's in March 1909, detailing terms for a volume of short stories that would include the short novel. He noted that work on this material has "diverted [James] from the novel, and delayed that. He tells me, however that he is now devoting himself entirely to the novel, and I shall hope to send it to you later in the year. This will be the American story which he has promised you [*The Ivory Tower*]."[173] *Harper's Magazine* editor Frederick Duneka replied with delicacy towards the author's request: "The publication of only one story, 'Julia Bride,' in a small book, will be received with greater favor by the public, and would sell more than a volume containing this as one of several other stories."[174]

Harper's had expressed interest in publishing the story as a volume in and of itself back in November 1906, and James's repeated attempts

---

[173] Ibid.

[174] Letters Sent to James B. Pinker Concerning Henry James.

to change the arrangement (publication after the long novel that had not and would never be completed, and now as part of a collection of short stories) long after Harper's desired publication date must have been frustrating for the editor, but his diplomacy eventually paid off and the author agreed to his terms. The publisher's original proposal of November 1906 claimed that "we cannot undertake to make any advance on royalty on this book,"[175] but three years later, when James finally allowed them to go forward as they wished, Duneka was "pleased to publish the story and to pay Mr. James a royalty of fifteen per cent, on the trade-list price of all copies sold, with advance on account of royalty of two hundred pounds on day of publication."[176] How this advance was obtained is unclear, but Pinker's usual machinations generally brought about the offering of advances that suited James's financial insecurities, so it would be safe to assume that the agent had something (or everything) to do with it.

Julia Bride was published by Harper's on September 25, 1909 in both America and England, but the long novel, due to be delivered by the end of the year (by Pinker's estimation), had yet to appear by the beginning of December. Duneka wrote Pinker on December 8 expressing the interest of the entire house, including George Harvey, in the book, with the hope that "we might have the privilege of seeing it."[177] James's Christmas Eve reply made it clear that no long novel would be forthcoming due to his ill health but a shorter novel had been started that might be suitable for Harper, and if so, "I will then ask my friend Mr. J.B. Penker to settle the matter of terms with you."[178] The editor remained cordial towards the author and his inconstant plans: "The book, as a book, it should seem,

---

[175] Ibid.

[176] Henry James Collection.

[177] Ibid.

[178] Archives of Harper & Brothers, 1817-1914.

would take care of itself, for one is always prepared for a good thing of that kind."[179] No 'good thing' came to Harper's from James, however, and *Julia Bride* would be the last of his works published by them. A year and a half later, in June 1911, Harper's turned down *The Outcry*, James's fictional account of his own play, and as noted previously, Scribner's accepted it for publication after this refusal.

Like Harper's, Chapman & Hall did not publish another James title, and wrote Pinker in 1913 and 1914 regarding unsold copies of *The American Scene*: "I am sorry to find that we still have 684 copies of Mr. Henry James's 'AMERICAN SCENE' unsold . . . I think the time has arrived when we must clear the stock."[180] In seven years, only a little over half of the 1500 copies printed had sold in England. While the publisher remained respectful and polite, their financial loss must have prevented them from offering to publish more of the author's material.

Pinker was certainly aware of James's lack of popularity and ensured his client's financial gain by insisting on advances that were not ultimately met by sales, including one for *Julia Bride*, which was at first to be published without an advance, according to the publisher's initial offer, but James ultimately received a rather large one for such a short novel. The agent was also able to convey James's distress at Harper's mistakes in the publication of *The American Scene* sufficiently to elicit an apology from the company president while maintaining the publisher's interest in continuing to issue James's work. The author's frustration with Harper's did not undermine his trust in his agent as he continued to keep his 'oar' out of the water in order to allow Pinker to manage the ongoing details of business transactions complicated by James's emotional reactions and the irritation of publishers left to wait on the author's unpredictable production habits and capricious

---

[179] Henry James Collection.

[180] Letters Sent to James B. Pinker Concerning Henry James.

disposition towards standing agreements.

Periodicals

Pinker was well used to the workings of periodicals, with prior experience as a reader, agent, correspondent, and editor for at least three before embarking on his career as a literary agent. His attempts to continue to keep James in front of the periodical readership during a time when that audience seemed to prefer to be entertained by action and adventure stories rather than the psychological drama and introspection James crafted were at least as difficult as those undertaken for book publication. While the agent was not daunted by continued refusals on James's behalf, he was less successful on this front than that of books, *The American Scene*, with its own attendant problems, notwithstanding.

James became acquainted with Pinker through the agent's work as assistant editor of *Black and White* in the early 1890s; the author contributed three stories, "Brooksmith," "The Real Thing," and "The Visit" to that publication in 1891 and 1892. His first approach to Pinker was in regard to the placement of three more stories, sent to the agent by James in the spring of 1898. The author had been having difficulty with the market for his work since the time of his *Black and White* submissions, primarily because editors found their readers more interested in shorter works of action rather than James's usual lengthy psychological studies. After over thirty years of generally easy placement of his material in periodicals (personal connections with editors such as William Dean Howells certainly helped), James was desperate. Pinker responded to James's direction to keep the three stories if the agent saw "any chance for them"[181] by finding a place and payment for all three: "The Given Case" appeared in *Collier's Weekly* in December 1898 and January 1899, and "Europe" and "The Great Good Place" appeared in *Scribner's Magazine* in June 1899 and January 1900 respectively.

James had enjoyed a long relationship with *Scribner's Monthly* that included the serial publication of his early novel *Confidence* (1879) and short stories, beginning with "Adina" in 1874. Pinker expected the magazine to continue to publish James's work and to pay well for the privilege. The possibility that he might not receive the requested amount for the author's material did not prevent him from asking for what he believed it was worth, making reference to the amount James's articles were bringing in from other publications. In September 1899, editor Edward Burlingame assured Pinker that "we cordially wish not to be behind others in paying Mr. James the best prices possible"[182] but the submitted piece, "Rye and Winchelsea," was rather short and did not merit the mentioned £75 that the *North American Review* was paying. He offered £40 but made it clear that he would remember the higher price James's longer articles were worth in the future. The editor did not just refuse to pay the higher amount; he qualified his decision as if it were necessary to explain the lower rate in order to prevent any offense to the agent or author.

Pinker successfully sold two more short stories for James to *Scribner's Magazine*, "The Tone of Time" (November 1900) and "Flickerbridge" (February 1902); the second would be the last of the author's short stories to appear in the magazine. Two weeks before "Flickerbridge"

---

[181] Horne, *Henry James: A Life* 310.

[182] Henry James Collection.

was submitted to the editor, James sent the last chapters of *The Sacred Fount* to Pinker but made it clear that the material "won't do for serialization."[183] While he was not explicit as to his reasons, the length and the subject matter would have made it difficult to sell as a serial, and at least he was able to recognize this and save the agent the trouble of attempting to sell it as such. It sold to Scribner's as a volume only, published in February 1901.

While Scribner's published two more of James's novels, *The Wings of the Dove* (1902) and *The Golden Bowl* (1904) they did not serialize either one, although James did make brutal cuts to the latter when Richard Gilder of the *Century* expressed interest, only to cable "Declined" upon receipt. The only James material published by Scribner's from 1905 to 1910 was the ill-fated New York Edition, which claimed so much of the author's time and effort with so little reward.

When James finished *The Outcry*, the publisher accepted it as a book but refused it as a serial. Pinker wrote that James "would be very pleased if it were possible for you to run it serially in Scribner's Magazine"[184] to no avail. He did not give up on the possibility and asked Scribner's to postpone publication until he could obtain assistance from American agent Paul Reynolds, one of the two agents (the other, Elisabeth Marbury) he used on occasion to assist in his North American efforts, as he did not have an office there. The publisher agreed and sent Reynolds a set of proofs, but unfortunately, the American agent had no more luck than Pinker. Scribner's conveyed the bad news to Pinker while insisting on a publication date as soon as possible, preferably the following month, October 1911, when in fact it was published. Pinker still held to the idea that a serial was possible and contacted the American agency of Curtis Brown & Massie in November to request

---

[183] Edel, *Henry James: Selected Letters* 322.

[184] Archives of Charles Scribner's Sons.

their assistance and received a response that was, while not necessarily hopeful, not dismissive: "We will see what proposal our clients can make with regard to Mr. Henry James's book, 'The Outcry,' and will write you as soon as we have their reply."[185] They were unsuccessful, unfortunately, and *The Outcry* was never serialized.

Scribner's published the three autobiographical books, *A Small Boy and Others*, *Notes of a Son and Brother*, and *The Middle Years*; Pinker had made an agreement with them to produce articles from the first two books in *Scribner's Magazine* but James's well-established and indulged habit of changing his work during the writing process regardless of how it was initially presented to and accepted by publishers ruined the agent's efforts: "We are obliged reluctantly to decide against them on the ground of their radical difference for our purposes," Burlingame wrote, because he believed that it was impossible to split up the material because of the "discursiveness" which was part of its charm (he was referring to *A Small Boy*). The writing itself made the editor "feel deeply" but was not by its nature able to be divided into separate articles, as it "could not as it seems to us have the same kind of value or be as justly understood."[186]

Originally the plan was to base the book on William James's letters to his brother, but the writing turned into more of an introduction to those letters, and that introduction grew into the second book, a development that concerned Charles Scribner, who wrote in October 1913 (seven months after the first volume was published) that he expected articles to come from the second volume as they had not been made from the first: "I fear that Mr. James's Introduction to the Letters has grown into a second volume and that the Letters themselves (which were expected to make the bulk of the volume) will not appear at all." He

---

[185] James B. Pinker and Son: Collection of Papers, 1893-1940.

[186] Letters Sent to James B. Pinker Concerning Henry James.

worried that "this enterprise is likely to prove disappointing if my fears are well founded" as "we started with the idea of a volume of William James's Letters and we shall have two volumes on Mr. James's early life." Scribner did not, however, want to trouble the author himself with this concern: "Of course this is for your eyes and I do not wish to discourage Mr. James,"[187] he insisted in his letter to Pinker.

James had strayed yet again, and while Scribner made it clear that he did not want to distress him, he was upset that the material had become something far different from what he expected and worse, unsuitable for the magazine. Pinker could negotiate terms and handle the technicalities of business arrangements but obviously had no control over James's actual writing activity, which was undermining the agent's ability to maintain avenues of publication for the work.

From the beginning of his working relationship with James, Pinker was undaunted by refusals and looked to publications that were not necessarily the most promising in order to place James's writing in print. In July 1898 he approached Harrison S. Morris, editor of *Lippincott's Monthly Magazine* (which featured Conan Doyle, Wilde, and Kipling) regarding James's short story "Maude Evelyn." The magazine had published essays by the author from 1877 to 1879 but had not expressed an interest in his material since, or in his fiction ever. It must not have surprised Pinker to receive a reply that noted the editor was "still in doubt about its adaptability to our needs on account of the great length,"[188] and whether or not it was the length or the requested payment, *Lippincott's* did not accept it.

Pinker moved on and distributed the stories in hand among the quality monthlies, and Bliss Perry, editor of the *Atlantic Monthly*, took

---

[187] Henry James Collection.

[188] Ibid.

"Maude Evelyn." The *Atlantic*, founded in 1824, had a reputation for printing the best fiction along with literary and social criticism, and had featured Harte, Hawthorne, Lowell, and Stowe. Perry published the story in April 1900 but his interest in James's work waned; he declined "The Faces," which appeared instead in *Harper's Bazar* in December 1900. "Maude Evelyn" would be the last James short story to appear in the *Atlantic*, while three of his biographical essays would be published in the magazine over the next fifteen years.

Perry's refusal to be forthcoming about his indifference to James's fiction caused problems for Pinker soon after the editor turned down "The Faces." Still encouraged by Perry's acceptance of "Maude Evelyn," Pinker sent Perry the synopsis of a novel James planned to write (which would become *The Wings of the Dove*) and Perry allowed that he would respond with an offer, although he was actually looking for material that would appeal to a wider, non-literary audience. After two months of waiting, an impatient James complained to Pinker in February 1900: "Will you kindly let me know if the *Atlantic* does *not* want my novel. I don't think that, in all the circumstances of our past relations, the editor (especially after refusing 'The Faces') should keep me a longer time in suspense - or be allowed to."[189]

In October 1899, James specifically told Pinker that he wanted to sell the novel as a serial as well as a book, but Perry finally returned the synopsis in May 1900 and *The Wings of the Dove* was never published serially. This refusal was a blow to James, who had seen his fiction serialized in the *Atlantic* since 1875 with *Roderick Hudson*. His first signed work, "The Story of a Year," had been published in the magazine in 1865. His long standing relationship with the publication was failing in part because of the new editor (who had a personal distaste for James's work) and the changing interests of periodical readership. James vented

____

[189] Vincec 68

to Howells on August 9, 1900, "The *Atlantic* declined [*Wings*] - saying it really only wanted 'Miss Johnston'!"[190] "Miss Johnston" was Mary Johnston, whose historical romance *To Have and to Hold* ran as a serial in the magazine in 1899, was published by the periodical's publisher, Houghton Mifflin as a volume in 1900, and became the best-selling novel in the United States that year.

James, anxious for the return of the *Wings* synopsis only months earlier, wrote with excitement to Pinker in May 1900 about a new work for which he would stop working on the still unnamed *Wings* for a time because "Harper and Brothers have within the last fortnight asked me for a serial (not *that* one - a different and special thing:) and I have said a general Yes."[191] Early in the next year, Pinker stepped in to formalize the details of the agreement; unbeknownst to him, the New York office of Harper's wanted the book but did not want to publish the serial in *Harper's Magazine* (which had a wide audience and a "cultural level slightly lower"[192] than its competitors, according to Frank Luther Mott) and instructed their London office to find a way to "relieve us of the serial use."[193]

Kaplan claims that Pinker made the arrangements for the serialization of the novel, which would be *The Ambassadors*, while Sedgwick notes that "through Howells, *The Ambassadors* was finally serialized by the

---

[190] Horne, *Henry James: A Life* 342.

[191] Vincec 66.

[192] Frank Luther Mott, *A History of American Magazines* (Cambridge: Belknap Press of Harvard UP, 1957-1968) 717-718.

[193] Henry James Collection.

flamboyant Col. George Harvey in the *North American Review*."[194] The agreement with the Harper magazine, which included a £2000 payment, was signed on May 22, 1901, and Pinker had the manuscript from the author in early July 1901. By June of the next year, however, Harper's had done nothing with it since receiving it in September 1901, and both James and Pinker were concerned; the two considered taking it back.

On January 3, 1903, James wrote Pinker: "I hear from Harper's, all of a sudden, that they are serializing 'the Ambassadors' after all, in the North American Review."[195] From January to December 1903, it appeared in twelve monthly installments and was the first fiction ever published in the magazine. The *Review* had been in print since 1815 and was known for its essays on art, history, social conditions (including slavery), and biography when Harvey purchased it in 1899. Harvey was operating at a loss and kept the magazine going for prestige, so while he was taking a chance on James he was used to losing money during those first few years.[196]

James made another attempt to have his work published in the *Review* in January 1904, when he asked Howells to approach Harvey on his behalf: "Will you kindly say to Harvey of me that I shall have

---

[194] Ellery Sedgwick, "Henry James and the Atlantic Monthly: Editorial Perspectives on James's 'Friction With the Market.'" *Studies in Bibliography: Papers of the Bibliographical Society of the University of Virginia* 45 (1992): 380. Harvey not only owned the *North American Review* but *Harper's Weekly* as well. He served as editor and president of Harper and Company from the turn of the century until 1915.

[195] Horne, *Henry James: A Life* 379.

[196] Colonel Harvey was also the reluctant but respectful publisher of Conrad: "I regard Mr. Conrad as a true genius and am proud to see the Harpers imprint upon anything he writes. But alas, I cannot compel the public to buy and, as you will readily perceive, we have not profited from these publications." Harvey to British author and critic (and frequent contributor to *Harper's Magazine* Sydney Brooks in 1910, quoted by S.W. Reid, "American Markets, Serials, and Conrad's Career." *The Conradian* 28 (2003): 64-65.

much pleasure in talking with him here of the question of something serialisable in the North American, and will broach the matter of an 'American' novel in *no* other way until I see him."[197] This came to nothing, but by that time Pinker had already negotiated with the editor regarding the series of articles and book of travel impressions based on James's upcoming trip to America, for either the *North American Review* or *Harper's Monthly*, which would be published as a volume as well.

The agreement was formalized in April 1904, and called for Harvey to publish at least eight installments at £80 each, and if more were wanted, they would be purchased at the same rate. The novel serialization depended on which magazine published it. Because *Harper's Magazine* circulated in England as well as America, the price was £1500, considerably more than the £500 payment for appearing in the *North American Review* (and leaving the English serial rights to the author).

James left for America four months after the agreement was signed; in October he wrote to Pinker expressing his confusion over the details, which, granted, were a bit complicated, and wondering which magazine would ultimately be the best financial bet, for although the *Review* paid less, Pinker might be able to sell it to an English magazine and bring in more than the £1000 difference in price if *Harper's* circulated it on both sides of the Atlantic. As usual, James counted on Pinker to keep the terms of the contract straight, although the author signed said contract himself.

While Pinker was handling the details of *The American Scene* serialization, Howells was assisting his friend by negotiating a series of lectures for the author during his travels, by which he could finance his trip. James was pleased at how well received he was in this medium. He wrote Pinker in March 1905: "I *have* done very well, for my material, my 'literary' situation & reputation, by my presence here these few

---

[197] Anesko, *Letters* 397.

months."[198] His bank account did very well, too; he earned $4050 in lecture fees during his journey. Elizabeth Jordan, editor of *Harper's Bazar* (which published "The Faces" in December 1900 after Perry at the *Atlantic* turned it down), was interested in a series of articles based on James's impressions of American women and wrote James and Pinker in July 1906 confirming her respect for the author and his work. She agreed to Pinker's request for £50 per article and wanted to be sure she had expressed her "full appreciation of my privileges in being able to publish these papers of yours" which would "do our women much good."[199]

Jordan's next letter confirmed that James would write specifically about the speech and manners of American women, and the one that followed two weeks later continued in its agreeableness and appreciation, explaining the specific schedule at which the articles would appear. James and Pinker's experience with Jordan and *Harper's Bazar* was a far cry from the one they suffered with *Harper's Magazine* and the *North American Review*, which was as frustrating as the book publication, detailed earlier. *Harper's Bazar* was, of course, quite a different publication from the other two, as it was a fashion magazine that extended its concern to manners and culture, as shown by Jordan's interest in James's observations and commentary on female manners and speech.

James wrote Harvey in January 1905 to make his preferences as to placement of the material known while explaining that the delay in writing the actual work was due to the abundance of material he had and was continuing to gather: "I shall greatly rejoice if you judge the North American Review to be the best place for my papers. As to this you will freely judge - but in the case (of the N.A.R.) I shall be able to

---

[198] Horne, *Henry James: A Life* 410.

[199] Henry James Collection.

have them placed, somehow, independently, in England."[200]

The *North American Review* published "New England: An Autumn Impression" as the first of the contracted installments in April and June 1905, sending full payment of £160 on March 25. In December of that year "New York and the Hudson" appeared. In January and February 1906, the *NAR* published "New York Social Notes" (also published in Chapman & Hall's *Fortnightly Review* in February), followed in March on both sides of the Atlantic by "Boston." In March Pinker made inquiries to the magazine as to the payment for the New York articles and was told that they had been submitted as a single piece but split into two by "Mr. Munro, for the sake of convenience"[201] and was paid as one, as originally presented to the magazine. Pinker did not manage to get the extra £80 for James, but it was not for lack of effort.

Three more installments, "Philadelphia" (April 1906, also in the *Fortnightly Review*), "Washington" (May and June 1906), and "Baltimore" (August 1906) followed in the *NAR* later in the year. The *Fortnightly Review*, known for publishing Trollope, Meredith, and Swinburne, had paid $873 in 1905 for four installments, and was concerned with keeping simultaneous publication with the *NAR*, while they had, in fact, only been delayed one month with "New York Social Notes" because of the length. The issue had been handled by the American publication by splitting it in two, but the *Fortnightly* held it over a month to publish in its entirety, as their January issue was "largely occupied with current politics."[202] Editor W.L. Courtney seemed to think the agent had some say as to the length of James's production, which was obviously untrue, and wrote Pinker to complain that it had caused a delay in publication.

Meanwhile, Pinker encountered more difficulties later that summer

---

[200] Horne, *Henry James: A Life* 408.

[201] James B. Pinker and Son: Collection of Papers, 1893-1940.

[202] Ibid.

when the publication timeline for the *NAR* appeared to be interfering with plans for the book issue. He wrote to Harper's (noted earlier) about the delay that would come about if the Florida article would be included in the volume. James was "most anxious" to avoid this, and wanted an autumn date for publication. In the midst of handling the American essays, the agent peddled unrelated James material in the fall of 1906, including "The Second House" and *Julia Bride*, both to Frederick Duneka at *Harper's Magazine*.

Duneka declined the short story, which would be published as "The Jolly Corner" in the *English Review* two years later, but accepted the short novel on the condition that Harper would have the book as well as serial rights, for which the editor gave $600, "which is more than we have ever paid for a short story by this distinguished author."[203] It was a long short story, rather a novella, but the offer was high and therefore acceptable regardless.

James's frustration over the treatment of his travel articles was growing, fed partially by his own confusion over the terms. The agreement specifically stated that Harper's would publish "no less than eight installments" but made no promise to publish more; James, however, was upset that two articles he had submitted, "Richmond" and "Charleston" were set aside and never appeared. Pinker wrote the *NAR* in the spring of 1907 to inquire about their failure to publish the two and was assured that while the pieces were indeed unable to be accommodated because of the space needed for other material, those that were published were paid for.

James was incensed by the response and complained to his agent, claiming that the letter "of which you sent me a copy deeply excited the wrath of even one of the most patient (as I claim for myself) of men" and focused on the fact that he had sent Mr. Munro notice of the articles

---

[203] Letters Sent to James B. Pinker Concerning Henry James.

he was submitting, and that the editor had held onto them without use, while they might have been placed elsewhere: "As it is, I extremely resent their whole indifferent, cavalier, uncivil treatment of my stuff, as if it were beneath their notice."[204]

The London office of Harper's sent a letter from Pinker detailing the problem to their New York office, which confirmed the information but did not know how to handle the situation, writing back to explain that they had just not had the room for the material in the magazine, and were "a little uncertain what is called for under the circumstances."[205] Pinker wrote to Mr. Slater at the London office that same month (May), reiterating the author's complaint that he should have been notified if the articles were "unwelcome."[206]

Harvey wrote James directly to apologize profusely for the perceived slight, nearly three months after Pinker's contact, reassuring him that no offense or disrespect was intended, and as Pinker requested, paid $350 for the unprinted "Charleston." James was still upset as the year came to a close, writing to Edith Wharton in November that "I am in no intimate relation at present with either the *Atlantic* or the *North American Review*, which latter has behaved very rudely and in fact offensively to me over the whole progress of my American papers."[207]

While Harper's was negotiating over the publication of *Julia Bride* (previously noted), Pinker used the publisher's disquiet and desire to keep James happy to attempt to make arrangements for two new short stories, "Crapy Cornelia" and "A Round of Visits" the next spring. In March 1909 he wrote stating that James wished for them to be serialized, then included in a volume along with *Julia Bride* and several other

---

[204] Archives of Harper & Brothers, 1817-1914.

[205] Letters Sent to James B. Pinker Concerning Henry James.

[206] Archives of Harper & Brothers, 1817-1914.

[207] Edel, *Henry James: Letters: 1895-1916* 475.

stories. Duneka insisted on publishing *Julia Bride* on its own, and "Crapy Cornelia" was published in *Harper's Magazine* in October that year, two months after *Julia*. The other stories James wanted included in a *Julia* volume were gathered together as a collection and published as *The Finer Grain* in 1910, not by Harper's but Scribner's.

Before Pinker offered the short stories he suggested Harper include in the *Julia Bride* volume, he approached *Putnam's Magazine* with two of them, "The Velvet Glove" and "The Bench of Desolation." The latter was the only James story to appear in that magazine, which, as the publisher of Longfellow, Melville, Lowell, Thoreau, and Cooper had a long-standing reputation as a highly literary production and at the time they published James, was focused on literary essays, poetry, and social news related to artists and writers. *Putnam's* expressed concern over the length of the stories in two letters to Pinker early in 1909, the first regarding "Bench," explaining that the payment would be based on the number of installments necessary, with £20 for a 4000 word story. It was published in four installments (October through December 1909 and January 1910), which presumably would have increased the payment.

In January 1910 James worried that he had yet to be compensated; ultimately, he was paid $218, or about £44 ("Bench" ran around 20,000 words, which would make this amount short by at least half of the expected payment). The second letter from *Putnam's* most likely concerns "The Velvet Glove," again referring to the length (11,000 words), this time as the cause for the magazine's refusal of the piece, noting that while they would be accepting of something "four, five, or even six thousand words in length" they did not expect that "from what you have told me, that so short a narrative will ever be available."[208]

---

[208] James B. Pinker and Son: Collection of Papers, 1893-1940.

Paul Reynolds, the American agent who had and would continue to assist Pinker on occasion, contacted the agent around the same time to offer his services in placing "The Velvet Glove" in America, and other stories, if available, as well. Whether Pinker accepted his offer or not, the story did not appear in America but only in England in the *English Review*, which James's friend Ford Madox Hueffer founded and was editing in March 1909.

James's personal connections had helped him place his material in the past, so he and Pinker (who was also Hueffer's agent) put his friendship with and the agent's work on behalf of the editor to use in 1908 and 1909, during which the *English Review* printed "The Jolly Corner" (declined by *Harper's Monthly* in 1906), "The Velvet Glove," and "A Round of Visits." There were no formal contracts between the editor and writer; James was paid the going rate of £50 to £75 according to length, and the author was satisfied until Hueffer's personal problems resulted in the loss of his control over the magazine in 1910.

A Mr. Peters from the magazine wrote Pinker in the summer of 1909 asking for copies of the agreements between James and the *English Review*, but such agreements did not exist. James was disappointed in the payment he received for "A Round of Visits," which appeared in April and May 1910; $97 (about £20) was considerably lower than what he was used to getting from the publication when his friend was in charge. Not surprisingly, this was the last of the author's work to appear in the *English Review*.

Pinker was not afraid to shame publishers, like Harper, into printing and paying for material even if terms were under contention (*The Ambassadors*) or misunderstood by the author (*The American Scene* essays), who was responsible for the acceptance of those same terms by his signature. As always, the agent managed to put money in the author's bank account upfront, before all terms of a contract (written or verbal) were satisfied (*Julia Bride*). Reynolds's (and others') failure to sell *The Outcry* as a serial and possibly "The Velvet Glove" speaks to the difficulty of placing James's work in general. Pinker's efforts to obtain publication for his client's material, both the short stories and serial installments of his novels, in periodicals were not discouraged, along with those regarding James's books, and were successful enough to keep the author in print intermittently and paid sufficiently, if not well, for it.

The Estate

When Stephen Crane died in June 1900, Pinker, who had been loyal to the author as agent and friend, felt no such devotion to Crane's self-styled widow, Cora. She begged for money (as Crane had done in order to support her) from those in Crane's literary circle, and after H.G. Wells made a donation, went "from him to Conrad and James, but Pinker, who knew her, was able to head them off from giving her full support."[209] The agent's concern for the benefactors of James's labors following the author's death in February 1916 was quite different. James's sister-in-law Alice, his brother William's widow, and in turn, her children, were granted James's property, including royalties, in his will and Mrs. James, satisfied with Pinker's handling of the author's affairs as much as she knew of them, kept him on as the literary agent of the estate, a role he continued to fulfill with the utmost regard for James's work.

Around the time James died, Pinker was testifying on behalf of his client D.H. Lawrence concerning *The Rainbow*, which had been declared obscene in November 1915. Pinker was understandably furious that the publisher involved, Methuen, caved in to pressure from a British magistrate who actually had no legal authority to make such a decision, and destroyed 1011 copies of the book rather than support the author,

---

[209] David C. Smith, *H.G. Wells: Desperately Mortal* (New Haven: Yale UP, 1986) 175.

who had Pinker's financial support "pretty much on demand."[210] He had also taken on another controversial author, James Joyce, which would have added not only to his workload but his stress level as well, as Pinker corresponded with the author, potential publishers, and Joyce's New York lawyer, John Quinn, who was defending the serial publication of *Ulysses*.

Pinker's emotional reaction to the Lawrence situation along with the death of one of his oldest clients most likely influenced his quick action on James's behalf soon after the author was buried. Edel notes that "the agent Pinker was aware of the way in which reputations can slip once a writer is dead; it was necessary to put the posthumous writing into print - the two unfinished novels, the autobiographical fragment, and finally the representative collection of the correspondence."[211] Less than two months after James's death, Pinker contacted Scribner to discuss three unfinished works left by the author: *The Sense of the Past*, *The Ivory Tower*, and *The Middle Years*. He also mentioned "his Letters," with immediate concern for arrangements for the editing of the same, and asked for the publisher's suggestions on how to best handle the publication of the material, specifically so he could discuss any offers with the James family.

Copies of the book manuscripts were already being made, Pinker explained, so all would be ready when the publication details were finalized. These copies were being made by James's secretary, Theodora Bosanquet, who had worked for the author from 1907 until his death. She wrote Pinker four days after his letter to Scribner with concerns about the fate of the unfinished work, recognizing that it was Pinker who was at the bottom of protecting James's memory: "I have reason to believe that it is entirely owing to your suggestion that copies are being

---

[210] Gillies 101.

[211] Leon Edel, Ed. *Henry James, Letters: 1843-1875* (Cambridge: Harvard UP, 1974) xx.

made at all, which is a fact that no one who cares for the preservation of his writings can be too grateful to you for."[212]

Pinker's next missive to Scribner in May 1916 included copies of the two incomplete novels and the letters along with a detailed description of their composition and his thoughts on how they ought to be published, with a sales pitch that displayed his intimate knowledge of James's work habits and his belief that there was, without a doubt, a market for the author's material based on the novelty of unfinished and revealing work by such a reserved figure. He offered "rough notes" for *The Sense of the Past* along with a "preliminary statement of the whole constructive idea, and another statement dealing with the plan for the novel [*The Ivory Tower*]" suggesting that both be published serially followed by book publication that would include the working material, not only to satisfy "natural curiosity as to the development of the stories, but for the reason that they are extremely fascinating to all who are interested in Mr. James' methods of work. Mr. James, as you know, never took the public into his confidence in the popular sense and revealed his methods."[213]

A little over a month later, Edward Burlingame wrote to settle the matter of the autobiographical piece, *The Middle Years*, "which had interested us very much and with regard to which we should be glad to make you a proposition for the Magazine - of course assuming the book use later in some form on the usual terms" but was noncommittal regarding the novels, claiming that the publisher had not yet decided how best to handle them. He offered $250 for "two very interesting and successful articles" made from *Middle*, to be published in early 1917. He agreed with Pinker about the importance of the unpublished material: "We are of course sincerely interested, as you are, in keeping

---

[212] Henry James Collection.

[213] Archives of Charles Scribner's Sons.

Mr. James's work together and in seeing what he has left used to the best advantage."[214]

Using the work to the best advantage for Mrs. James was what the agent had in mind when he composed his response, asking for £100 (about $475) per article, to which the publisher cabled "Think our offer adequate but will give Three Hundred Dollars each for two articles."[215] Pinker replied immediately in agreement, without consulting Mrs. James, taking the higher sum although lower than his suggestion, and in turn received a promise to publish not only the two articles but also the entirety of the material as a volume. His authority in such matters, whether given explicitly by Mrs. James or implied, was clear. The articles were published in *Scribner's Magazine* in October and November 1917, concurrent to the book issue. Payment of $600 as offered by the publisher was received and acknowledged by Pinker on November 17, 1916. In the letter that accompanied the check, Burlingame confirmed the expectation of book publication, assuring Pinker that "we shall be very glad to undertake the book issue."[216]

Pinker took several weeks to respond, with good reason and a push to settle the matter of the unfinished novels in the manner he had originally suggested. He had been discussing the editing of the same with Percy Lubbock, a friend and admirer of James and a writer in his own right, who was unable as yet to determine anything about the handling of the author's correspondence, but would be able to write "a short note" for each novel about its origin. Pinker asserted that each novel should be published as its own volume, with Lubbock's notes as well as those of James on the development of each: "I think published in that way they would be valued by everyone who was interested in

---

[214] Henry James Collection.

[215] Archives of Charles Scribner's Sons.

[216] Ibid.

Henry James's method of work."[217]

Burlingame, however, did not agree, and his answer, which came two months later, stated that the two should be issued in one volume, with "some editorial accompaniment" and "could be called by some title showing that it contained Mr. James's unfinished work." He *did* agree to Pinker's request for the usual 20% royalty, but to the agent's question of an advance ("I find it difficult to suggest what would be appropriate in the way of advance") he did not believe that "we should be asked for an advance in this case."[218] Pinker knew that an advance was unnecessary, as unnecessary now as it had been vital while the author was living, and did not press the point.

The contracts he drafted, however, detailed his own expectations for the production of the novels as noted in his own letter, disregarding the editor's thoughts, reiterating that each book should be its own volume, claiming that the composition sketches would add enough to the length of each to make them substantial: "I have had a cable from Mrs. William James entirely approving this plan, and I feel sure that you too will approve it."[219] He could not possibly be sure, as Burlingame had stated less than two months earlier that he certainly did *not* approve. "We are still inclined to think that publication of the two in one volume will be the most practicable shape for us," the editor explained in response, but was more forceful on another matter he had brought up earlier that made no appearance in the Pinker draft. He wanted to be sure that Lubbock's editing fee would be split between Scribner's and the English publisher, and that was a point that had to be made in the contract before he could sign.

The publication date would become an issue only because of the

---

[217] Ibid.

[218] Ibid.

[219] Ibid.

American involvement in the war, and the coming publishing season would be, to put it mildly, "uncertain."[220] Burlingame expected that it would be put off from the autumn (the letter was dated May) but believed the following year would be possible. Pinker revised the contracts to please Burlingame on account of the editing fee and returned them, with Mrs. James's signature, to the editor on July 24, 1917. *The Sense of the Past* and *The Ivory Tower* were published in separate volumes, identical in appearance, on October 17, 1917, despite the editor's warning about the probability of later publication, primarily because both novels were also published in England by Collins on September 6, 1917.

Pinker had been corresponding with William Collins & Sons regarding an English edition of the works to be published by Scribner's and made arrangements that were acceptable to Alice James: "It seems to be a very advantageous arrangement. I am thankful to have the books well made, 'well produced' as you say."[221] The Scottish publisher specialized in religious and educational texts but with the promotion of Godfrey Collins started publishing fiction in 1917 with James, the "Grand Literary Panjandrum" who had "enjoyed great prestige" followed by "public indifference."[222]

Collins editor Gerald O'Donovan was considerate of his American counterpart and the need to provide proofs for their use as soon as possible, assuring Pinker in June 1917 that the material would be in his hands by the end of that month to pass along to Scribner's, making a fall publication on both sides of the Atlantic possible. Burlingame was not pleased with these plans and reminded the agent of the war concerns while noting that simultaneous publication was "essential

---

[220] Ibid.

[221] Ibid.

[222] David Keir, *The House of Collins* (London: Collins, 1952) 236.

for all reasons; so that the decision of the English publishers virtually forces us to issue the books in the autumn also." While the editor was unhappy with this turn of events, he was even more worried about the fate of the articles from *The Middle Years*, which could not be published in the magazine until the fall: "We shall rely upon you to safeguard us with the English publishers."[223]

Collins was to publish the autobiographical work as well, and releasing it in England before the American serial would be a death-dealing blow to any profit for Scribner's. Burlingame seemed to believe that Pinker should be acting on behalf of Scribner's, when the agent was not and never had been in the business of 'safeguarding' publishers. He was, in all cases, his author's agent, and would continue to be so during this transaction. Pinker responded to Burlingame's concerns with contracts on July 24, Lubbock's completed prefaces in August, and beginning that same month, corrected proofs from Collins for all three titles.

Publication of the novels is previously noted; *The Middle Years* was published by Collins on October 18 while Scribner's printed from copies sent by Pinker two weeks prior to produce the American edition on November 23. In February 1918 Pinker had to remind Scribner's of their obligation to Lubbock: "I shall be very much obliged if you will let me have a cheque for the fee due to Mr. Percy Lubbock in payment of his work of editing the Henry James books."[224] A check was sent on March 19.

Six weeks later, the agent offered Scribner's another opportunity to print James, with previously published articles on war collected in a volume entitled *Within the Rim*, for which Pinker had made arrangements with Collins to publish that autumn. He explained that

---

[223] Archives of Charles Scribner's Sons.

[224] Ibid.

the material was gathered at the "request of many friends" and were "the last things that Mr. James wrote, and the only written comments that he has left on the War, so that they will have permanent interest for his friends."[225] This began a series of correspondence that revealed either hesitation or disinterest on the part of the publisher.

Pinker gave Scribner's the price that Collins was asking for providing the sheets for American printing, but Burlingame was concerned because he did not know what the list price would be for the book in England, so the asking price for sheets could not be judged in its reasonableness since it was based on the list amount. He also wanted Collins to pay the royalties to the James estate for any American sales. Collins agreed to this stipulation, and Pinker gave the editor the price of the book, but Burlingame was still unsatisfied, finally reaching his point of contention at the end of his last correspondence on the matter. He claimed that the "little collection of war papers" was "attended with difficulties," and the price he would have to ask American consumers to pay would be extravagant for such a small volume, if it were to be of any profit: "Now that the war is over and there has come decided reaction against war books, the outlook even for the Henry James collection of war papers is not particularly encouraging."[226] *Within the Rim* was published in the United Kingdom in March 1919; Scribner's refusal meant that no American edition would follow.

Pinker's April 1916 letter in which he presents James's unfinished work to Scribner made brief mention that "there will be besides these his Letters." No further notice of these letters came from the agent, who was occupied with the novels and autobiography; seven months later, Burlingame, concerned by information gleaned from correspondence with the author's nephew, wrote Pinker to inquire about them: "what

---

[225] Ibid.

[226] Ibid.

we hear from London friends of Mr. James (and here since Mrs. William James's return) seems to show that the matter of the Letters has been arranged with Mr. Percy Lubbock."[227] He was concerned that he had not been made aware of developments regarding the letters, although the publisher had expressed interest in them as a collection and wanted to use them in their magazine as well. Pinker explained that there was nothing to report regarding the letters, hence his silence. Lubbock was busy with work on the novels, and would be for some time, and in December 1916 Pinker told Burlingame that Lubbock "tells me that it is too early yet to say anything usefully definite as to the Letters."[228]

Five months later, the agent wrote Burlingame as if Scribner's had not expressed a definite interest in the letters, possibly to let him know that there might be competition (although there is no evidence of any) if negotiations did not go as Pinker saw fit: "I have had a proposal this morning from America for the publication of the Letters, first in magazine and afterwards in volume form. The proposal is not a detailed one, and I am simply postponing the matter, but I shall be glad if you and Mr. Scribner will consider the question of publishing some of the correspondence in the magazine."[229] The tone of Pinker's missive must have set Burlingame understandably on edge, but resulted in the definite agreement to publish that Pinker was after, one that included magazine publication. Burlingame insisted: "you know of course from our repeated inquiries that we are looking forward with warmest interest to having their publication in book form; and we will willingly say definitely what in our November letter we mentioned our hope to arrange, that we will make a proposal to publish some considerable portion of them in the Magazine." He again expressed his hope that the

---

[227] Ibid.

[228] Ibid.

[229] Ibid.

publisher could "rely on your not making any arrangements elsewhere until the whole matter shall have been fully discussed between us."[230]

Nearly two years passed before the letters became an object of concern once again, after Lubbock had finished his work on them and Pinker had made arrangements with Macmillan to publish the English edition. Pinker wrote Scribner's in June 1919 to explain an unforeseen delay caused by a mishap the letters had suffered during travels with James's nephew, during which some of the chapters "have gone astray and I am now compelled to wait until I can get a set of proofs from Macmillans."[231] Burlingame seemed to take the news well, writing to Pinker that he was looking forward to receiving the proofs, but he wrote in turn to Macmillan, immediately, with a complaint about the delay, asking the English publisher to "send copies of any preliminary announcements you are making with regard to the book."[232] Frederick Macmillan agreed to send one after it had been drawn up and supported Pinker's claim about the delay in providing proofs against Burlingames's complaint, assuring him that they would be sent along "as soon as they have been corrected by the Editor, Mr. Percy Lubbock."[233]

Macmillan wanted to publish the letters that fall but understood that the approval of all the parties involved, after Lubbock's work was complete, might cause further delay, writing Pinker in September: "I presume that Mr. Lubbock will not pass them for press until he is satisfied that Mrs. James passes them. It certainly looks as if it may be necessary to hold the book over until the turn of the year, but I hope that this will not be so."[234] The completed proofs of the first volume, passed

---

[230] Ibid.

[231] Ibid.

[232] Ibid.

[233] Ibid.

[234] Henry James Collection.

by Lubbock, made their way to Macmillan and finally to Scribner's in the middle of November; Macmillan had yet to inform the American publisher of the price and date of publication, but assured Scribner's that they would do so "later on."[235]

While Scribner's attempted to obtain proofs and information from Macmillan, Pinker was arranging with Scribner for the articles based on the letters, suggesting in October 1919 that Edmund Gosse would be well suited to the work, in his own opinion and that of James's nephew, "since from his long friendship with Mr. Henry James he would have resources to draw upon apart from the Letters."[236] Pinker sent the first article to Scribner on December 8, 1919, asking when the publisher intended to print it. The reply indicated that Scribner had either misunderstood or forgotten the details of the October letter, particularly that of Gosse's ability to write about James outside of the information in the letters: "While we appreciate the skill with which Mr. Gosse has prepared his first article, we are frankly disappointed that it contains so little in the way of extracts and material from the remarkable letters." They had "expected the letters of Henry James with comments by Mr. Gosse"[237] and the second article, sent less than a month later, met their satisfaction. Payment of £100 was sent to Pinker for Gosse, the agreed upon amount.

Pinker continued to have difficulty reaching terms with Scribner's; the contract with Macmillan had been settled over six months before he wrote to Scribner's in January 1920 asking for an agreement, as Macmillan had sent proofs and was asking for March publication. If this was not possible, Macmillan "thought it would not matter their being a little ahead of you," but if Scribner's considered "it important

---

[235] Archives of Charles Scribner's Sons.

[236] Ibid.

[237] Henry James Collection.

that the two editions should be simultaneous I shall be glad if you will cable so that I can stop Macmillans."[238] Whether Pinker would have actually made an effort to change the English publication date to suit Scribner's is unlikely, but his need to finalize the financial end of the transaction satisfactorily led him to make the situation as agreeable to Scribner's as possible, even if it meant extending an offer he would not be able or willing to deliver.

Macmillan contacted Scribner's less than a week later to inform them of their intentions: "We propose to publish the book here on Tuesday, March 9th, and trust that this date will not be inconvenient to you."[239] Macmillan changed the date less than two weeks later: "We find however that this date will be inconvenient and we shall therefore postpone the appearance of the book until Friday, April 9th, a date which we trust will be convenient to yourselves."[240] This letter crossed one from Scribner's to Pinker regarding the first date: "Agree to simultaneous publication of James book March twenty-sixth immediately after appearance of first Gosse article."[241] This one crossed, in turn, one from Pinker to Scribner's regarding the revised dates: "Sir Frederick Macmillan has fixed April 9th for the publication here of the Henry James Letters. He tells me that from the correspondence he has had with you he is sure that you can copyright by then."[242] Scribner's settled the matter with a cable to Macmillan on February 26: "Agree to April ninth simultaneous publication James Letters."[243]

Pinker was still waiting on an agreement with terms for the letters,

---

[238] Archives of Charles Scribner's Sons.

[239] Ibid.

[240] Ibid.

[241] Ibid.

[242] Ibid.

[243] Ibid.

which now had a definite publication date in both countries that was exactly a month away when the American publisher cabled the English one to obtain their price in order to arrive at an offer for Pinker. A week before publication, Pinker's son Eric sent a contract to Scribner: "I have drafted the agreement for the Henry James letters [standard 20%] and have pleasure in sending it to you, herewith."[244] The letters were published by Macmillan on April 8 and Scribner's on April 9; the contract was signed by Scribner's and returned to the agent on April 21.

While James was living, Pinker had considered the publication of another collected edition, one that might sell better than the New York Edition by virtue of a lower price. He contacted Scribner's in 1915 to see if they had any objections; more likely than not, he was actually concerned about any legal barriers to this plan and informing the publisher ahead of time would reveal any issues before he began to work on it. The agent had not yet brought the idea to James's attention but was acting of his own accord, explaining to Scribner that "it is only an idea of mine" and he "imagined that that would not interfere with your sale." He had "not mentioned the matter to Mr. James because I did not know whether it were possible or advisable."[245]

Before the agent returned to the idea of a 'new' collected edition after the author's death, he approached Scottish publisher Thomas Nelson and Sons in March 1917 about issuing several James titles, which was what the August 1915 letter to Scribner described, albeit as a set. Nelson was interested in *Roderick Hudson*, *Daisy Miller*, *The Bostonians*, *The Princess Casamassima*, *The Tragic Muse*, and *The Madonna of the Future*; they were concerned, however, with the variety of publishers involved

---

[244] Ibid.

[245] James B. Pinker and Son: Collection of Papers, 1893-1940.

in the original production of these titles, and asked if Pinker would supply copies of each from which they would print their own. Pinker was happy to oblige, and having already been through the drama of securing permissions, reassured Nelson, and their edition was printed from 1918-1920.

With Nelson complete, Pinker moved on to present the notion of a 'popular' edition to Macmillan before returning to Scribner in 1919, telling the American publisher that Macmillan would include all the volumes in the New York Edition as well as others thought "desirable." He asked for Charles Scribner's "views on the subject" as well as his interest in issuing the set in America, which would, in the agent's estimation, be offered fifty cents cheaper per volume than the New York Edition: "It would involve making fresh arrangements with the publishers who are interested in the Henry James books in America, but I wanted to ascertain your views before going any further."[246] Pinker did not seem to be concerned about the 'fresh arrangements' and after all, he had been through the process before and knew now what to expect and how to handle it. His expression of interest in Scribner's 'views' is not necessarily sincere; the agreement with Macmillan was signed by Alice James and returned on September 10, 1919, before Scribner responded to Pinker's August letter. The correspondence from Macmillan to Scribner during this time makes no mention of the popular edition, either because the focus of the communication was the James letters or because Pinker suggested discretion on Macmillan's part.

Scribner's seemed amenable to the plan and open to printing an American edition if Macmillan agreed to make it worth their while financially, as they had invested a great deal of time and effort into their edition, which all involved knew did not sell well. Supplying the

---

[246] Archives of Charles Scribner's Sons.

English publisher with sheets or duplicate plates was one way to recoup some of their costs, and if Macmillan was open to an offer for the use of the same, Scribner's "should be favorable to bringing out such a new edition particularly if our plates can be used as we are suggesting."[247] Unfortunately, Macmillan was not interested in using the New York Edition plates and gave his reasons to Pinker, listing the size of the page as well as the use of books not included in the New York Edition as prohibitions to an agreement.

Scribner's had addressed the page size in their offer, claiming that the "type-page could be used on a very much smaller book" so Macmillan's protest seems like an effort to find an excuse to refuse, rather than outright stating that he did not want to pay Scribner's, much as Scribner had made negotiations difficult for Pinker in regard to *In the Rim* based on disinterest. Three days after Macmillan wrote Pinker, the agent passed the news on to Scribner, repeating Macmillan's concerns asking Scribner if the publisher would want to "approach the other publishers regarding permissions, or for me to do so?"[248] Scribner's held firm to the use of their plates as a prerequisite to obtaining their blessing and participation in the edition, and of course, told Pinker to do the work of gathering permissions for an American edition himself. They were worried about the use of the New York Edition prefaces as well, as "they were of course written for the New York Edition and we think they should only be used in connection therewith." The cheaper edition might be "directly competitive" with the older issues of the books, Scribner's warned, and the original publishers "might wish to hold us up for a considerable payment"[249] for such reason.

Scribner's appealed directly to Macmillan in January 1920 regarding

----

[247] Ibid.

[248] Ibid.

[249] Ibid.

the James letters and made mention of the popular edition to see how the project stood, as they had not received a reply to their last letter to Pinker of November 1919, noting that the agent had informed them that the use of their plates "seemed impossible." Macmillan maintained a short and firm refusal: "We are obliged to you for your offer of the plates of your New York Edition of Mr. Henry James's novels for use in printing our contemplated Collected Edition. We regret to say however that we cannot avail ourselves of it."[250] The American publisher finally revealed their main concern and objection to the edition, which was no surprise but could have been set forth more directly from the beginning of the conversation but was overshadowed by the possibility that they might profit by Macmillan's use of the plates.

The English publisher's refusal to cooperate with Scribner's on the matter pushed Scribner's to come clean about their fears in April: "I think it would be distinctly injurious to the New York Edition if a more complete uniform edition of the fiction were issued through the trade." Adding to the New York Edition, as Macmillan wished to add titles not included in that edition to the cheaper one, was something Scribner's was open to discussing, but mention of such a collaboration had not been made. The whole matter, Scribner's reminded Pinker, "depends on the consent of other publishers."[251]

The tables turned the next month when Frederick Macmillan discovered that there was an arrangement made by Pinker that might affect his plans to publish James and wrote to ask the agent's assistance to maintain what he believed was an exclusive right to the work: "I am rather concerned to see in 'The Publisher's Circular' of last week an advertisement of a cheap edition of Henry James's Roderick Hudson to be published by Nelsons." He asked Pinker to "look into this matter at

---

[250] Ibid.

[251] Additional Letters Concerning the James Family.

once,"[252] unaware that the agent himself had been a party to the Nelson publication. Pinker's interest was, of course, limited to the James estate and did not extend to acting on Macmillan's behalf unless the estate stood to benefit.

The Nelson negotiations had taken place in early 1917, and the Macmillan primarily in 1919, the latter without knowledge of the Nelson agreement. Eleven years earlier, Frederick Macmillan had written James in response to the author's request that *The American* be allowed print in Nelson's Sevenpenny Library: "We will voice no objection to the publication."[253] His blessing clearly did not extend to other titles over a decade later. Pinker's answer to Macmillan's query brought more concerns forth from the publisher, who was "rather horrified" to be informed that at least six of James's "best books" would be published by Nelson's: "It seems to us to alter the whole complexion of our own enterprise in the Henry James domain."[254] The complexion, as it were, of the popular edition was unaltered, however, and while Scribner's refused to participate with an American edition, Macmillan published *The Stories and Tales of Henry James* between January 1921 and November 1923. Whatever obstacles had been set before him, Pinker fulfilled his idea of a cheaper collected edition that was initially considered in 1915, an endeavor he had originally contemplated without the author's knowledge or consent.

Acting on his own was clearly something Pinker believed part of his job, and while James had been interested to an extent in his business dealings he was content to allow his agent to manage without his approval to specifics unless a problem arose; this, in Pinker's estimation, was to

---

[252] James B. Pinker and Son: Collection of Papers, 1893-1940.

[253] Ibid.

[254] Charles Deering McCormick Library of Special Collections.

be avoided at nearly all costs. Alice James entrusted Pinker quite as much, allowing the agent to "decide such applications, always from the standpoint of the author's interest. I feel sure that you and I are agreed in considering all such attempts to 'produce' Henry James solely from the point of view of his own interest. I mean that I would not allow his work to be treated as insignificant."[255] Her trust in Pinker was a reflection not only of her brother-in-law's experience with him but her own as well. There is no mention of money in her letter; her reliance on the agent is specific as to the treatment of James's work as valued material worth perpetuating. She knew that Pinker would continue to strive to keep the author's work in print for the right price, a price based not on her desires but on the merit of the work. Her regard for Pinker was based on his own for James's work, which was demonstrated as he continued to negotiate with and between publishers for the best placement of the author's unpublished work after his death, serving the memory and legacy as well as he had the man.

---

[255] Additional Letters Concerning the James Family.

A Bet on the Side of Literature

When Pinker died in 1922, six years after James, he had spent the last twenty-four years of his life in the service of at least seventy-five authors. His dedication to James in particular, which was rivaled only by his attention to Joseph Conrad and Stephen Crane insofar as difficulty of their personalities and work habits, resulted in the publication of eight novels, several collections of short stories and essays, three autobiographical volumes, over sixty contributions to periodicals, and the Collected Edition. Pinker's ability to provide a business service personalized to James's temperament ("my own stuff done in my own way") and working habits allowed the author to continue to produce material; James's tendency to overreact and respond quickly and emotionally to difficulties would have easily disrupted his writing process.

Without Pinker to reassure James that business arrangements were moving along successfully, regardless of the truth, and with the 'down' (advance) in the author's pocket to assuage James's ever present financial fears, James would not have been able to focus on his writing and might very well have stopped writing publishable work altogether. A failure to produce on James's part would not have affected Pinker financially, as he had married into financial security and had no need to concern himself with sales to his benefit.[256] The connection between Pinker's efforts and James's continued presence before the public (not without its financial ends, necessary to satisfy the author's insecurities about his economic situation) is demonstrated through the agent's handling of the negotiations between the author and his publishers during the last eighteen years of James's life. He did not work for James alone during these years, but had a full roster of clients of varying personal and professional needs that make his efforts for James all the more impressive, as does the complete lack of any documented complaints Pinker made about anyone, to anyone, spoken or in writing. It is difficult to believe that he took everything in stride, but true to professional form, he may have saved the venting of such a stressful career for the home and hearth.

James's habit of moving from publisher to publisher, chasing the best placement and price for his work before hiring Pinker to handle his business affairs, placed the agent in the midst of a difficult situation from the start. He was, however, not intimidated by editors and publishers, such as Heinemann, who disliked agents for this same behavior, nor did he refer to James's practice of doing so prior to their relationship. He was also not afraid to continue the author's practice when and if it served the author and the material best. Publishers such as Methuen did not appreciate this but did value Pinker's ability to handle the author when James did not produce material by the contracted delivery dates, even if that 'handling' was limited to ensuring that James continued to write, with no promise of completion.

The agent could "muffle" business troubles for James to maintain the author's creative cocoon, which, while catering to and in effect,

---

[256] This is not to say that Pinker married for money. Stape relates that Pinker met Mary when her coach collided with his bicycle, landing him in a ditch. Her father did not approve of the resulting romance, and the pair married within months of his death two years after they met.

condoning James's self-centered work habits, kept the author working. Methuen and Scribner's both complained to Pinker that any delay during the production process was due to James; the agent never acknowledged any fault by the author to the publishers nor did he admonish James in any regard. He begged for indulgence on behalf of James to extend deadlines and get advances prior to publication in order for James to have money in hand so that he felt financially secure. When James wrote Pinker in 1900 at the beginning of their business relationship regarding *The Sacred Fount* that "the down" was important, Pinker clearly took it to heart and kept it in mind when managing future negotiations. He focused on details that ensured that author received all the royalties that were his due when Scribner's failed to send the correct payment amount for *The Golden Bowl,* and expressed his and the author's distress over an unauthorized reprint that had no bearing on his finances but was instead a matter of allowing the author to determine the appropriate placement for his material.

Until the New York Edition was published, James was earning more than double the money yearly he was making before employing Pinker. This expensive (for all parties involved) stumbling block took all of the agent's patience and ingenuity; his efforts, while gaining the author a higher percentage of royalties than originally offered, did not offset the failure of the Edition to sell and make a substantial return over and above the permissions payment Scribner's covered, which was to be repaid through royalties. While James was devastated by this outcome, he did not seem to blame his agent, who had assured him that the Scribner's to Macmillan payment would not come out of his royalties. He appears to have accepted the bad with the good in consideration of Pinker's work on his behalf, and finding that primarily, Pinker was a blessing. "I wanted particularly to get Mr. James all that I can on this book" was Pinker's bottom line, and even if the financial aspects did not work out as Pinker and James wished, at least James was still in print.

Even after the author's death, the agent continued to fulfill the wishes of the estate and James's heir, Alice James, in presenting unfinished material left by the author in the best manner possible, as Mrs. James was concerned primarily that her brother in law's work would be well produced and respected.

Pinker did not look for personal fame or fortune but rather the perpetuation and preservation of James's work. He accepted the author as he was without trying to change him in order to make his own job easier, and played an integral part in James's life during a time when the author's work did not meet popular demand and expectations, a situation that created numerous difficulties for the agent. He consistently used firm diplomacy to encourage existing and potential publishers to accept the proposed material along with terms that suited James, allowing for negotiation when it served the interest of keeping James in print. When James was obviously at fault for causing difficulties for his publishers, Pinker ignored or redirected their complaints and refused to accept blame on his client's behalf; nor did he ever admonish James for his refusal to adhere to contractual delivery dates or content as originally accepted by the publisher.

There is no evidence that Pinker ever complained about James in any regard. His role was to advocate for James alone; unlike some other agents, who worked in their own best interest, serving publisher and agent in order to preserve their own future prospects, he cared little, if at all, for how publishers saw him except as one who would settle for nothing less than what would serve his client. At times he bargained for publication when financial gain was less than probable (the Collected Edition) and at others, settled James with a well-padded bank account before the publisher had even glimpsed the work (*The American Scene*), resulting in a loss to the publisher.

Many factors contributed to the difficulties Pinker found in finding publishers for James's materials, not the least of which were the changing preferences of a growing audience of readers and the author's work habits. Competing with the "Miss Johnstons" of the market was not within James's abilities as a writer or a businessman, as demonstrated during the final decade of the nineteenth century. James may have continued to produce material without Pinker to assist him on the business aspect of his profession, but without the agent, he probably would not have been able to place as much of it or for as much financial profit, profit that came primarily in the form of advances insisted upon by the agent, which of course had nothing to do with sales figures but was rather a guarantee of payment upfront.

With a temperament easily upset and frustrated by setbacks, his writing may have been stifled and come to a halt as he attempted to find time and energy to negotiate with publishers in an effective and non-alienating manner. His approach to Pinker in 1898, and the agent's decision to "bet on the side of literature" knowing that this prospective client was on popular decline, forged the business relationship that would keep James writing and his continued work in print for the rest of his life and Pinker's thereafter. As a prime example of Howells's 'man of letters' in an era of business, James could neither profane his art by "fashioning it upon fashion" nor could he escape the financial need (real or psychological) to make a living from his writing.[257]

Pinker served James in order to reconcile these contradictory issues and allow the author to fulfill Howells's - and clearly James's - own belief that the writer should write what pleases him most, producing material that forges connections with readers through real and honest representations of life rather than popular (dated) entertainment. The interest in James and his work over the past eighty years proves the value of the author's work across time; without Pinker's mediation, the

---

[257] William Dean Howells, "The Man of Letters as a Man of Business," *Literature and Life (Complete)* (2006) 2-18, Literary Reference Center, EBSCO, 24 Sept 2011.

material produced over the last eighteen years of James's life, including that which has been produced in Hollywood film and television series versions within the last twenty years, might have remained in the author's notebook and imagination.

Publications by Henry James, late
1898-1923

12/1898-01/1899
   The Given Case
   Collier's Weekly* (American)

04/1899
   The Awkward Age
   Heinemann (English)

05/1899
   The Awkward Age
   Harper & Brothers (American)

06/1899
   The Great Condition
   Anglo-Saxon Review* (English)

06/1899
   Europe
   Scribner's Magazine* (American)

09/1899
  Two Old Houses and Three
  Young Women
  The Independent* (American)

10/1899
  The Present Literary Situation in France
  North American Review* (American)

12/1899
  Paste
  Frank Leslie's Popular Monthly* (American)

12/1899
  The Real Right Thing
  Collier's Weekly* (American)

01/1900
  The Great Good Place
  Scribner's Magazine* (American)

01/1900
  The Letters of Robert Louis Stevenson
  North American Review* (American)

04/1900
  Maud Evelyn
  Atlantic Monthly* (American)

05/1900
  Miss Gunton of Poughkeepsie
  Cornhill Magazine* (English)

05-06/1900
  Miss Gunton of Poughkeepsie
  The Truth* (American)

06/1900
  The Special Type
  Collier's Weekly* (American)

08/1900
  The Soft Side (short stories)
  Methuen (English)

09/1900
  The Soft Side (short stories)
  Macmillan (American)

11/1900
  The Tone of Time
  Scribner's Magazine* (American)

12/1900
  Broken Wings
  Century Magazine* (American)

12/1900
  The Faces
  Harper's Bazar* (American)

01/1901
Winchelsea, Rye, and Denis Duval
Scribner's Magazine* (American)

02/1901
The Sacred Fount
Charles Scribner's Sons (American)

02/1901
The Sacred Fount
Methuen (English)

03/1901
Matilde Serao
North American Review* (American)

08-09/1901
Mrs. Medwin
Punch* (English)

10/1901
The Beldonald Holbein
Harper's New Monthly Magazine* (American)

11/1901
Edmond Rostand
Cornhill Magazine* (English)

11/1901
Edmond Rostand
The Critic* (American)

01/1902
  The Story in It
  Anglo-American Magazine* (Canadian)

02/1902
  Flickerbridge
  Scribner's Magazine* (American)

04/1902
  George Sand: The New Life
  North American Review* (American)

08/1902
  The Wings of the Dove
  Charles Scribner's Sons (American)

08/1902
  The Wings of the Dove
  Archibald Constable (English)

01-12/1903
  The Ambassadors
  North American Review* (American)

02/1903
  The Better Sort (short stories)
  Methuen (English)

02/1903
  The Better Sort (short stories)
  Charles Scribner's Sons (American)

08/1903
   Emile Zola
   Atlantic Monthly* (American)

09/1903
   The Ambassadors
   Methuen (English)

10/1903
   William Wetmore Story & His Friends
   William Blackwood (English)

10/1903
   William Wetmore Story & His Friends
   Houghton, Mifflin (American)

11/1903
   The Ambassadors
   Harper & Brothers (American)

04/1904
   Gabrielle d'Annunzio
   Quarterly Review* (English)

11/1904
   The Golden Bowl
   Charles Scribner's Sons (American)

12/1904
   Fordham Castle
   Harper's Magazine* (American)

02/1905

The Golden Bowl
Methuen (English)

04-06/1905

New England - An Autumn Impression
North American Review* (American)

08/1905

The Question of Our Speech
Appleton's Booklovers Magazine* (American)

08/1905

The Lesson of Balzac
Atlantic Monthly* (American)

10/1905

The Question of Our Speech (lectures)
Houghton, Mifflin (American)

10/1905

English Hours (essays)
Heinemann (English)

10/1905

English Hours (essays)
Houghton, Mifflin (American)

12/1905

New York and the Hudson: A Spring Impression
North American Review* (American)

01/1906
  New York: Social Notes. I
  North American Review* (American)

02/1906
  New York: Social Notes. I
  Fortnightly Review* (English)

02/1906
  New York: Social Notes. II
  North American Review* (American)

02-03/1906 & 05/1906
  New York Revisited
  Harper's Magazine* (American)

03/1906
  Boston
  North American Review* (American)

03/1906
  Boston
  Fortnightly Review* (English)

04/1906
  Philadelphia
  North American Review* (American)

04/1906
  Philadelphia
  Fortnightly Review* (English)

05-06/1906
Washington
North American Review* (American)

08/1906
The Sense of Newport
Harper's Magazine* (American)

08/1906
Baltimore
North American Review* (American)

11/1906
Richmond, Virginia
Fortnightly Review* (English)

11/1906-02/1907
The Speech of American Women
Harper's Bazar* (American)

01/1907
The American Scene (essays)
Chapman & Hall (English)

02/1907
The American Scene (essays)
Harper & Brothers (American)

04-07/1907
The Manners of American Women
Harper's Bazar* (American)

12/1907-07/1909
The Novels and Tales of Henry James (The New York Edition)
Charles Scribner's Sons (American)

09/1908-1909
The Novels and Tales of Henry James (Edition de Luxe)
Macmillan (English)

03-04/1908
Julia Bride
Harper's Magazine* (American)

05/1908
Views and Reviews (essays)
Ball (American)

06/1908
The Married Son
Harper's Bazar* (American)

12/1908
The Jolly Corner
English Review* (English)

01/1909
An American Art-Scholar: Charles Eliot Norton
Burlington Magazine* (English)

03/1909
The Velvet Glove
English Review* (English)

08-09/1909
Mora Mortravers
English Review* (English)

09/1909
Julia Bride
Harper & Brothers (American)

10/1909
Italian Hours (essays)
Heinemann (English)

10/1909
Crapy Cornelia
Harper's Magazine* (American)

10/1909-01/1910
The Bench of Desolation
Putnam's Magazine* (American)

11/1909
Italian Hours (essays)
Houghton, Mifflin (American)

01-02/1910
Is There Life After Death
Harper's Bazar* (American)

04-05/1910
A Round of Visits
English Review* (English)

10/1910

The Finer Grain (short stories)
Charles Scribner's Sons (American)

10/1910

The Finer Grain (short stories)
Methuen (English)

10/1910

The Outcry
Methuen (English)

10/1911

The Outcry
Charles Scribner's Sons (American)

04/1912

A Letter to Mr. Howells
North American Review* (American)

07/1912

The Novel in The Ring and the Book
Quarterly Review* (English)

03/1913

A Small Boy and Others
Charles Scribner's Sons (American)

04/1913

A Small Boy and Others
Macmillan (English)

06/1913
Balzac
The Times Literary Supplement* (English)

08/1913
Balzac
The Living Age* (American)

03/1914
The Younger Generation
The Times Literary Supplement* (English)

03/1914
Notes of a Son and Brother
Charles Scribner's Sons (American)

03/1914
Notes of a Son and Brother
Macmillan (English)

04/1914
George Sand
Quarterly Review* (English)

06/1914
George Sand
The Living Age* (American)

10/1914
Notes on Novelists (essays)
Dent (English)

10/1914
  Notes on Novelists (essays)
  Charles Scribner's Sons (American)

07/1915
  Mr. and Mrs. Fields
  Cornhill Magazine* (English)

07/1915
  Mr. and Mrs. Fields
  Atlantic Monthly* (American)

1915-1920
  The Uniform Tales of Henry James
  Martin Secker (English)

05/1917
  The Uniform Tales of Henry James
  Le Roy Phillips (American)

08/1917
  Within the Rim
  Fortnightly Review* (English)

09/1917
  Within the Rim
  The Living Age* (American)

09/1917
  The Ivory Tower
  W. Collins (English)

09/1917

The Sense of the Past
W. Collins (English)

10/1917

The Middle Years
W. Collins (English)

10/1917

The Ivory Tower
Charles Scribner's Sons (American)

10/1917

The Sense of the Past
Charles Scribner's Sons (American)

10/1917

The Middle Years
Scribner's Magazine* (American)

11/1917

The Middle Years
Charles Scribner's Sons (American)

12/1917

Within the Rim
Harper's Magazine* (American)

11/1918

Gabrielle de Bergerac
Boni & Liveright (American)

03/1919

Within the Rim (essays)
W. Collins (English)

04/1919

Travelling Companions (short stories)
Boni & Liveright (American)

01/1920

A Landscape Painter (short stories)
Scott & Seltzer (American)

04/1920

The Letters of Henry James (selected and edited by Percy Lubbock)
Charles Scribner's Sons (American)

04/1920

The Letters of Henry James (selected and edited by Percy Lubbock)
Macmillan (English)

11/1920

Master Eustace (short stories)
Thomas Seltzer (American)

1921-1923

The Novels and Stories of Henry James
Macmillan (English)

04/1921

Notes and Reviews (essays)
Dunster House (American)

Bibliography

Primary Sources

Archives of Harper & Brothers, 1817-1914. Teaneck, NJ: Chadwyck-Healy, 1980.

Archives of Charles Scribner's Sons, 1786-2003. Department of Rare Books and Special Collections, Princeton University Library.

Henry James Collection. Yale Collection of American Literature, Beinecke Rare Book and Manuscript Library.

James B. Pinker and Son: Collection of Papers, 1893-1940. Berg Collection of English and American Literature, The New York Public Library.

James B. Pinker Additional Letters Concerning the James Family. MS Am 2540. Houghton Library, Harvard University.

Letters Sent to James B. Pinker Concerning Henry James. MS Am 1237.14. Houghton Library, Harvard University.

Pinker, James B. Charles Deering McCormick Library of Special Collections. Northwestern University Library.

Secondary Sources

"Agents – James B. Pinker." *Literary Year-Book and Bookman's Directory* 1901. 118

Anesko, Michael. "Ambiguous Allegiances: Conflicts of Culture and Ideology in the Making of the New York Edition." *Henry James's New*

York Edition: the Construction of Authorship. Ed. David McWhirter. Stanford: Stanford UP, 1995. 77-89

Anesko, Michael. *Friction with the Market: Henry James and the Profession of Authorship.* New York: Oxford UP, 1986.

Anesko, Michael. "James in America: In Quest of (the) Material." *Cambridge Quarterly* 37 (2008): 3-15.

Anesko, Michael. *Letters, Fictions, Lives: Henry James and William Dean Howells.* New York: Oxford UP, 1997.

The Bookman (death of J.B. Pinker, sons to carry on business) May 1922: 274-275.

Burlingame, Roger. *Of Making of Many Books: A Hundred Years of Reading, Writing and Publishing.* New York: Scribner, 1946.

Carabine, Keith. "Conrad, Pinker, and Under Western Eyes: A Novel." *Conradian* 10 (1985): 144-153.

Donovan, Alan B. "My Dear Pinker: The Correspondence of Henry James with His Literary Agent." *Library Gazette* 36 (1961): 78-88.

Duffy, Maureen. *A Thousand Capricious Chances: A History of the Methuen List, 1889-1989.* London: Methuen, 1989.

Edel, Leon, ed. *Henry James, Letters: 1843-1875.* Cambridge: Harvard UP, 1974.

Edel, Leon, ed. *Henry James, Letters: 1895-1916.* Cambridge: Harvard UP, 1984.

Edel, Leon, ed. *Henry James: Selected Letters.* Cambridge: Harvard UP, 1987.

Edel, Leon. *The Life of Henry James: The Treacherous Years, 1895-1901.* New York: Lippincott, 1969.

Edel, Leon and Dan Laurence. *A Bibliography of Henry James.* 2nd Ed. London: Hart-Davis, 1961.

Finkelstein, David. "James Brand Pinker." *Oxford Dictionary of National Biography.* Ed. H.C.G. Matthew and Brian Harrison. Vol. 44. Oxford: Oxford UP, 2004. 370-371.

Ford, Ford Madox. *Return to Yesterday*. New York: Liveright, 1932.

Gale, Robert L. "Henry James." *Dictionary of Literary Biography: American Realists and Naturalists*. Detroit: Gale, 1982. 297-326.

Gard, Roger. *Henry James: The Critical Heritage*. New York: Barnes & Noble, 1968.

Gillies, Mary Ann. *The Professional Literary Agent in Britain: 1880-1920*. Toronto: U of Toronto P, 2007.

Guy, Josephine M. and Ian Small. *Oscar Wilde's Profession: Writing and the Culture Industry in the Late Nineteenth Century*. Oxford: Oxford UP, 2000.

Hepburn, James. *The Author's Empty Purse & the Rise of the Literary Agent*. London: Oxford UP, 1968.

Hepburn, James, ed. *Letters of Arnold Bennett Volume 1: Letters to J.B. Pinker*. London: Oxford UP, 1966.

Holland, Merlin and Rupert Hart-Davis, eds. *The Complete Letters of Oscar Wilde*. London: Fourth Estate, 2000.

Howells, William Dean. "The Man of Letters as a Man of Business." *Literature & Life (Complete)* (2006): 2-18. *Literary Reference Center*. EBSCO. Web. 24 Sept. 2011.

Hunt, Violet. *I Have This to Say: The Story of My Flurried Years*. New York: Boni and Liveright, 1926.

"James B. Pinker Dies Here." *New York Times* 10 Feb. 1922: 13

Kaplan, Fred. *Henry James: The Imagination of Genius: A Biography*. Baltimore: Johns Hopkins UP, 1999.

Keir, David. *The House of Collins*. London: Collins, 1952.

"Literary Agent's Death." *(London) Daily Mail* 10 Feb. 1922: 5

Mackenzie, Norman and Jeanne. *H.G. Wells: A Biography*. New York: Simon, 1973.

Matthiessen, F.O. and Kenneth B. Murdock, Eds. *The Notebooks of Henry James*. New York: Oxford UP, 1955.

Mizener, Arthur. *The Saddest Story: A Biography of Ford Madox Ford*.

New York: Carroll, 1985.

Monteiro, George. "The Atlantic Monthly's Rejection of 'The Pupil': An Exchange of Letters Between Henry James and Horace Scudder." *American Literary Realism* 23 (1990): 75-83.

Moore, Rayburn S. "Henry James and 'The Pinker of Agents,' James B. Pinker." *PostScript: The Publication of the Philological Association of the Carolinas* 9 (1992): 85-90

Mott, Frank Luther. *A History of American Magazines*. Cambridge: Belknap Press of Harvard UP, 1957-1968.

O'London, John. "London Book Talk." *New York Times* 5 Mar. 1922: 58

Reid, S.W. "American Markets, Serials, and Conrad's Career." *The Conradian* 28 (2003): 57-99.

Sedgwick, Ellery. "Henry James and the Atlantic Monthly: Editorial Perspectives on James's 'Friction With the Market." *Studies in Bibliography: Papers of the Bibliographical Society of the University of Virginia* 45 (1992): 311-332.

Smith, David C. *The Correspondence of H.G. Wells, Volume 2: 1904-1918*. London: Pickering, 1998.

Smith, David C. *H.G. Wells: Desperately Mortal*. New Haven: Yale UP, 1986.

St. John, John. *William Heinemann: A Century of Publishing, 1890-1990*. London: Heinemann, 1990.

Stape, J.H. "Pinker of Agents: A Family History of James Brand Pinker." *The Conradian* 34 (2009): 111-143.

Swinnerton, Frank. *Background With Chorus*. London: Hutchinson, 1956.

Taylor, Linda J. *Henry James, 1866-1916, a Reference Guide*. Boston: G.K. Hall, 1982.

Vincec, Stephanie, C.S.J. " '*Poor Flopping Wings*': The Making of Henry James's The *Wings* of the Dove." *Harvard Library Bulletin* 24 (1976): 60-

93.

West, James L. *American Authors and the Literary Marketplace Since 1900*. Philadelphia: U of Pennsylvania P, 1988.

Wexler, Joyce Piell. *Who Paid for Modernism?: Art, Money, and the Fiction of Conrad, Joyce, and Lawrence*. Fayetteville: U of Arkansas P, 1997.

Whyte, Frederic. *William Heinemann, A Memoir*. Garden City, NY: Doubleday Doran, 1929.

Works Consulted

Aiken, Joan. *The Haunting of Lamb House*. New York: St. Martin's, 1991.

Baines, Jocelyn. *Joseph Conrad: A Critical Biography*. London: Weidenfeld and Nicolson, 1960.

Barnes, John. "Henry Lawson and the 'Pinker of Literary Agents.'" *Australian Literary Studies* 23 (2007): 89-105.

Beerbohm, Max. "Jacobean and Shavian." *Henry James: A Collection of Critical Essays*. Ed. Leon Edel. Englewood Cliffs, NJ: Prentice-Hall, 1963. (original print 2/27/09). 18-26.

Bell, Ian F.A. "The Jamesian Balloon: Romancing the Marketplace." *Journal of American Studies* 24 (1990): 351-368.

Benkovitz, Miriam J. *Frederick Rolfe: Baron Corvo*. New York: Putnam, 1977.

Berg, A. Scott. *Max Perkins: Editor of Genius*. New York: Riverhead, 1978.

Birch, Brian. "Henry James: Some Bibliographical and Textual Matters." *Library* 20 (1965): 108-123.

Bonham-Carter, Victor. *Authors by Profession, Volume One*. Los Altos: Kaufmann, 1978.

The Bookman Nov 1904: 195.

The Bookman (death of J.B. Pinker) Mar 1922: 96.

The Bookman (visitors to New York from England, including Messrs. Pinker) June 1925: 502.

Borus, Daniel H. *Writing Realism: Howells, James and Norris in the Mass Market*. Chapel Hill: U of North Carolina P, 1989.

Boulton, James T., ed. *The Selected Letters of D.H. Lawrence*. Cambridge: Cambridge UP, 1996.

Calder, Robert. *Willie: The Life of W. Somerset Maugham*. London: Heinemann, 1992.

Charvat, William. *The Profession of Authorship in America 1800-1870: The Papers of William Charvat*. Columbus: Ohio State UP, 1968.

Cloy, John D. *Pensive Jester: The Literary Career of W.W. Jacobs*. Lanham, MD: UP of American, 1996.

Colby, Robert A. "Harnessing Pegasus: Walter Besant, 'The Author,' and the Profession of Authorship." *Victorian Periodicals Review* 23 (1990): 111-120.

Colby, Robert A. " 'What Fools Authors Be!' The Author's Syndicate, 1890-1920. *Library Chronicle of the University of Texas at Austin* 35 (1986): 60-87

Collis, Maurice. *Somerville and Ross: A Biography*. London: Faber and Faber, 1968.

Conrad, Jessie. *Joseph Conrad and His Circle*. 2nd ed. Port Washington: Kennikat, 1964.

Cook, Emma. "Under Stress, Underpaid – The Unknown Henry James." *The Independent(London)* 30 May 1999. Web. 12 April 2010.

Core, George. "Author and Agency: Galsworthy and the Pinkers." *Library Chronicle of the University of Texas at Austin* 6 (1973): 61-73

Coustillas, Pierre, ed. *London and the Life of Literature in Late Victorian England: The Diary of George Gissing, Novelist*. Lewisburg: Bucknell UP, 1978.

Cronin, John. *Somerville and Ross*. Lewisburg: Bucknell UP, 1972.

Culver, Stuart. "Ozymandias and the Mastery of Ruins: the Design of the New York Edition." *Henry James's New York Edition: the Construction of Authorship*. Ed. David McWhirter. Stanford: Stanford UP, 1995. 39-57

Curle, Richard. *The Last Twelve Years of Joseph Conrad*. London: Sampson, Low, Marston, 1928.

Doran, George. *Chronicles of Barabbas, 1884-1934*. New York: Harcourt, 1935.

Dupee, F.W. *Henry James*. New York: Doubleday, 1956.

Dupre, Catherine. *John Galsworthy: A Biography*. New York: Coward, McCann & Geoghegan, 1976.

Edel, Leon. "The Architecture of Henry James's New York Edition." *New England Quarterly* 24 (1951): 169-178.

Edel, Leon. *The Life of Henry James: The Master, 1901-1916*. New York: Lippincott, 1972.

Edel, Leon and Gordon N. Ray, eds. *Henry James and H.G. Wells*. Westport: Greenwood, 1958.

Edel, Leon and Lyall H. Powers, eds. *The Complete Notebooks of Henry James: The Authoritative and Definitive Edition*. New York: Oxford UP, 1987.

Edel, Leon and Lyall H. Powers, eds. "Henry James and the *Bazar* Letters." *The Bulletin of the New York Public Library* 62 (1958): 75-103.

Edgar, Pelham. *Henry James, Man and Author*. Boston: Houghton Mifflin, 1927.

Eliot, Simon. "Some Trends in British Book Production, 1800-1919." *Literature in the Marketplace: Nineteenth-Century British Publishing and Reading Practices*. Ed. John O. Jordan and Robert L. Patten. Cambridge: Cambridge UP, 1995. 19-43.

The English Catalogue of Books. London: S. Low, Marston. 1835-1968.

Feltes, N.N. *Literary Capital and the Late Victorian Novel*. Madison: U of Wisconsin P, 1993.

Ferguson, Alfred R. "The Triple Quest of James: Fame, Art, and

Fortune." 1986. *On Henry James: The Best from American Literature.* Ed. Louis J. Budd and Edwin H. Cadey. Durham, NC: Duke UP, 1990. 53-76

Finkelstein, David. *The House of Blackwood: Author-Publisher Relations in the Victorian Era.* University Park: Pennsylvania State UP, 2002.

Firth, John. "James Pinker to James Joyce, 1915-1920." *Studies in Bibliography: Papers of the Bibliographical Society of The University of Virginia, Volume 21.* Charlottesville: The UP of Virginia, 1968. 205-224.

Fitch, Noel Riley. *Sylvia Beach and the Lost Generation.* New York: Norton, 1983.

Flower, Newman, ed. *The Journals of Arnold Bennett, 1911-1921.* London: Cassell, 1932.

Fritschner, Linda Marie. "Literary Agents and Literary Traditions: The Role of the Philistine." *Paying the Piper: Causes and Consequences of Art Patronage.* Ed. Judith Huggins Balfe. Urbana: U of Illinois P, 1993.

Gatrell, Simon. "The Collected Editions of Hardy, James, and Meredith, With Some Concluding Thoughts on the Desirability of the Taxonomy of a Book." *The Culture of Collected Editions.* Ed. Andrew Nash. New York: Palgrave Macmillan, 2003. 80-94.

Geoffroy-Menoux, Sophie. "Henry James and Family: Eleven Unpublished Letters." *Sources* 14 (2003): 6-111.

Gettman, Royal A., ed. *George Gissing and H.G. Wells: Their Friendship and Correspondence.* London: Hart-Davis, 1961.

Goldring, Douglas. *Trained for Genius: The Life and Writings of Ford Madox Ford.* New York: Dutton, 1949.

Graham, Kenneth. *Henry James, a Literary Life.* New York: St. Martin's, 1994.

Grattan, C. Hartley. *The Three Jameses: a Family of Minds: Henry James, Sr., William James, Henry James.* London: Longmans, 1932.

Haralson, Eric and Kendall Johnson. *Critical Companion to Henry*

James: A Literary Reference to His Life and Work. New York: Facts on File, 2009.

Harris, Marie P. "Henry James, Lecturer." *American Literature* 23 (1951): 302-14.

Hart-Davis, Rupert. *Hugh Walpole: A Biography*. New York: Macmillan, 1952.

Hart-Davis, Rupert, ed. *The Letters of Oscar Wilde*. New York: Harcourt, 1962.

Hastings, Selina. *The Secret Lives of Somerset Maugham: A Biography*. New York: Random, 2010.

Hayes, Kevin J., Ed. *Henry James: The Contemporary Reviews*. New York: Cambridge UP, 1996.

Hennegan, Alison. "Personalities and Principles: Aspects of Literature and Life in Fin-de-Siecle England." *Fin de Siecle and Its Legacy*. Ed. Mikulas Teich and Roy Porter. Cambridge: Cambridge UP, 1990. 170-215

Henry James. Ed. John Delaney. *Dictionary of Literary Biography Documentary Series* 13. Detroit: Gale Research, 1995. 314-321.

Herrick, Robert. "A Visit to Henry James." *Yale Review* 12 (1923): 724-741.

Hewitt, Rosalie. "Henry James, The Harpers, and The American Scene." *American Literature* 55 (1983): 41-47.

Hicks, Priscilla Gibson. "A Turn in the Formation of Henry James's New York Edition: Criticism, the Historical Record, and the Siting of The Awkward Age." *Henry James Review* 16 (1995): 195-221.

Hochman, Barbara. "Disappearing Authors and Resentful Readers in Late-Nineteenth Century American Fiction: the Case of Henry James." *ELH* 63 (1996): 177-201.

Hochman, Barbara. *Getting at the Author: Reimagining Books and Reading in the Age of American Realism*. Amherst: U of Massachusetts P, 2001.

Holly, Carol. "The Emotional Aftermath of the New York Edition." *Henry James's New York Edition: the Construction of Authorship*. Ed. David McWhirter. Stanford: Stanford UP, 1995. 77-89

Horne, Philip. "Henry James and the Cultural Frame of the New York Edition." *The Culture of Collected Editions*. Ed. Andrew Nash. London: Palgrave Macmillan, 2003. 95-110.

Horne, Philip. "Revising and Revisions in the New York Edition of the Novels and Tales of Henry James." *A Companion to Henry James*. Ed. Greg W. Zacharias. Malden, MA: Wiley-Blackwell, 2008. 209-230.

Hyde, H. Montgomery. *Henry James at Home*. London: Methuen, 1969.

James Brand Pinker. Obituary. *The Times (London)* 9 Feb 1922.

James, Elizabeth, Ed. *Macmillan: A Publishing Tradition*. New York: Palgrave, 2002.

James, Henry. Letter to William Heinemann. 2 Nov. 1984. Rpt. in *Hound and Horn* 7 (Apr/June 1934): 415.

Johanningsmeier, Charles. *Fiction and the American Literary Marketplace: the Role of Newspaper Syndicates in America, 1860-1900*. Cambridge: Cambridge UP, 2002.

Kaplan, Amy. *The Social Construction of American Realism*. Chicago: U of Chicago P, 1988.

Karl, Frederick R. and Laurence Davies, eds. *The Collected Letters of Joseph Conrad*. New York: Cambridge UP, 1983.

Karl, Frederick R. "Conrad and Pinker: Some Aspects of Correspondence." *Journal of Modern Literature* 5 (1976): 59-78

Kermode, Frank. "The Changing Profession of Letters." *Bulletin of the American Academy of Arts & Sciences* 36 (1983): 13-28

Kreyling, Michael. *Author and Agent: Eudora Welty and Diarmuid Russell*. New York: Farrar, 1991.

Labor, Earle, ed. *The Letters of Jack London: Volume Two: 1906-1912*. Stanford: Stanford UP, 1988.

"Literary Agent's Estate." (*London*) *Times* 28 Mar. 1922: 15

"London Book Talk." *New York Times* 5 March 1922, p. 58

Lubbock, Percy, Ed. *The Letters of Henry James.* New York: Scribner, 1920.

Ludwig, Richard M., ed. *Letters of Ford Madox Ford.* Princeton: Princeton UP, 1965.

Lukes, Bonnie L. *Soldier's Courage: the Story of Stephen Crane.* Greensboro: Morgan Reynolds, 2002.

McDonald, Peter D. *British Literary Culture and Publishing Practice, 1880-1914.* New York: Cambridge UP, 1997.

Mackenzie, Compton. *My Life and Times, Octave Five: 1915-1923.* London: Chatto, 1965.

Margolis, Anne T. *Henry James and the Problem of Audience: An International Act.* Ann Arbor: UMI, 1985.

Matthiessen, F.O. *Henry James: The Major Phase.* New York: Oxford UP, 1944.

Moore, Rayburn S., Ed. *The Correspondence of Henry James and the House of Macmillan, 1877-1914.* Baton Rouge: Louisiana State UP, 1993.

Morgan, Ted. *Maugham.* New York: Simon, 1980.

Murry, J. Middleton., Ed. *Journal of Katherine Mansfield.* London: Constable, 1927

Murry, John Middleton, Ed. *Katherine Mansfield's Letters to John Middleton Murry: 1913-1922.* New York: Knopf, 1951

Nowell-Smith, Simon. *The Legend of the Master.* New York: Scribner's, 1948.

O'Sullivan, Vincent and Margaret Scott, Eds. *The Collected Letters of Katherine Mansfield: Volume One.* Oxford: Clarendon, 1984.

Page, Norman. *Henry James: Interviews and Recollections.* New York: St. Martin's, 1984.

Parker, Hershel. "Henry James 'In the Wood': Sequence and Significance of His Literary Labors, 1905-1907." *Nineteenth-Century Fiction*

38 (1984): 492-513.

Powers, Lyall H. *Henry James and Edith Wharton, Letters: 1900-1915.* New York: Scribner's, 1990.

Putnam, George Haven. *Memories of a Publisher, 1865-1915.* New York: Putnam, 1915.

Read, Forrest, Ed. *Pound/Joyce: The Letters of Ezra Pound to James Joyce, with Pound's Essays on Joyce.* New York: New Directions, 1967.

Roderick, Colin, Ed. *Henry Lawson Letters: 1890-1922.* Sydney: Angus, 1970.

Rose, Jonathan. "Modernity and Print I: Britain 1890-1970." *A Companion to the History of the Book.* Ed. Simon Eliot and Jonathan Rose. Malden, MA: Blackwell, 2007.341-353.

Scoble, Christopher. *Fisherman's Friend: A Life of Stephen Reynolds.* Tiverton: Halsgrove, 2000.

Seymour, Miranda. *A Ring of Conspirators: Henry James and His Literary Circle, 1895-1915.* Boston: Houghton, 1989.

Sheehan, Donald. *This Was Publishing: A Chronicle of the Book Trade in the Gilded Age.* Bloomington: Indiana UP, 1952.

Simon, Linda. *The Critical Reception of Henry James: Creating a Master.* Rochester, NY: Camden, 2007.

Smith, David C. *The Correspondence of H.G. Wells, Volume 1: 1880-1903.* London: Pickering, 1998.

Stallman, R.W. and Lillian Gilkes, Eds. *Stephen Crane: Letters.* New York: New York UP, 1960.

Standish, Robert. *The Prince of Storytellers: The Life of E. Phillips Oppenheim.* London: Davies, 1957.

Stape, J.H. and Owen Knowles. " 'In-Between Man': Conrad – Galsworthy – Pinker." *Conradian* 31 (2006): 48-63.

Storrs, Ronald. *The Memoirs of Sir Ronald Storrs.* New York: Arno, 1972.

Swinnerton, Frank. *Authors and the Book Trade.* New York: Knopf,

1932.

Swinnerton, Frank. *Swinnerton: An Autobiography*. New York: Doubleday, 1936.

Szcypein, Jean M. "Joseph Conrad's 'A Personal Record': Composition, Intention, Design: Polonism." *Journal of Modern Literature* 16 (1989): 3-30

Thring, G. Herbert. *The Marketing of Literary Property*. London: Constable, 1933.

Tintner, Adeline. *The Twentieth-Century World of Henry James: Changes in His Work After 1900*. Baton Rouge: Louisiana State UP, 2000.

Towheed, Shafquat, Ed. *The Correspondence of Edith Wharton and Macmillan, 1901-1930.* New York: Palgrave Macmillan, 2007.

Tredrey, F.D. *The House of Blackwood, 1804-1954: The History of a Publishing Firm*. Edinburgh: Blackwood, 1954.

Troy, Michele K. "The Heuffer Brothers and the Artistic Temperament." *Journal of Modern Literature* 26 (2003): 28-46.

Turner, Linda. *Henry James, 1866-1916, a Reference Guide*. Boston: G.K. Hall, 1982.

Waller, Philip. *Writers, Readers, and Reputations: Literary Life in Britain 1870-1918*. Oxford: Oxford UP, 2006.

Walsh, Keri, Ed. *The Letters of Sylvia Beach*. New York: Columbia UP, 2010.

Waugh, Arthur. *A Hundred Years of Publishing: Being the Story of Chapman & Hall, Ltd.* London: Chapman, 1930.

West. Anthony. *H.G. Wells: Aspects of a Life*. New York: Random, 1984.

White, Edmund. *Hotel de Dream: A New York Novel*. New York: Ecco, 2007.

Wilson, Harris, ed. *Arnold Bennett and H.G. Wells: A Record of a Personal and a Literary Friendship*. Urbana: U of Illinois P, 1960.

Worthern, John. *D.H. Lawrence: A Literary Life*. New York: St. Martin's, 1989.

Wright, Harold, Ed. *Letters of Stephen Reynolds*. Richmond: Hogarth, 1923.

Young, Jessica Brett. *Francis Brett Young: A Biography*. London: Heinemann, 1962.

Zara, Louis. *Dark Rider: A Novel Based on the Life of Stephen Crane*. London: Joseph, 1962.

About the Author

Kerry Sutherland has a Master's degree in Library and Information Science and a PhD in English with an emphasis in American Literature from Kent State University. Her studies have been published in The Henry James Review, ANQ: A Quarterly Journal, Bearing Witness: Joyce Carol Oates Studies, and Progressive Librarian. She is a public services librarian in Northeast Ohio.